SECRETS OF THE LIMITLESS MIND

SECRETS OF THE LIMITLESS MIND

Authored by

YOGENDRA SINGH RATHORE

Penman Books

Office No. 303, Kumar House Building,
D Block, Central Market, Opp PVR Cinema,
Prashant Vihar, Delhi 110085, India
Website: www.penmanbooks.com
Email: publish@penmanbooks.com

First Published by Penman Books 2020
Copyright © Yogendra Singh Rathore 2020
All Rights Reserved.

Title: Secrets of the Limitless Mind
Price: ₹499 | $ 9
ISBN: 978-93-89024-79-1

Introduction

As I grew up in my hometown, and watched the closest people to me grow and change, there were so many questions that I had to ask which I ended up keeping to myself; and as time passed and I gather more questions and thoughts, I began to see a trend, a very obvious one, through the different issues and questions.

And when I became old enough to think for myself, and seek knowledge from around the world to make me wiser, I realized things that I considered very complex, and even impossible, were matters I could easily explain with one word- Mind.

So, what is the Mind?

A perusal through the Merriam Webster Dictionary of English Language will furnish us with a glimpse of what the mind entails. It defines the mind as "the element or complex of elements in an individual that feels, perceives, thinks, wills, and especially reasons; the organized conscious and unconscious adaptive mental activity of an organism."

In simpler, more direct terms, the mind is the real sense of being alive; the seat of a human existence that controls every other parts; from his feelings, to his perception, his thoughts, and his decisions. I dare say that it is this mind that decides a human's present, and shapes his future whether such human realizes it- consciously, or doesn't- unconsciously.

In the few decades I have spent in this world, there are some vital truths I have picked up from here and there, whether from books I have read, words of wise men I have listened to, or the lives of men I have studied. And I have found that the most consistent thing, the most frequent difference between humans; both the failed and the successful, the happy and the despondent, the great or the destitute, the one thing that separates one group from the other is the Mind, and how it was used.

How do you use your mind? How does your mind work? What goes on in your mind? What are some of your most prevailing thoughts? What do you believe? What do you think about? How do you use your mind?

Which begs the question: Do we even use the mind? Do we know we can use and master it? Do we understand it? An obvious answer to the last question will be No, we don't understand the man. And those who understand it don't do so enough. For a human who understands the mind and realizes it has no limit, is already on the way to perfect happiness and absolute fulfillment.

Hence, we have to ask ourselves, why don't we understand the Mind?

The answer to this important question is the same answer you would give if asked why you do not understand rockets; because you have not been trained to understand it.

If we consider a rocket to be so complex, that we must train people for years before they can be able to control it, why is it then that we don't have training classes for something as complicated as the mind?

Even something as simple as a radio set, or a mobile phone, when we acquire them, we get short users' manual that instructs us on how to use the gadgets. A washing machine also comes with a user manual, a computer does too. Even the food condiment, Maggie comes with steps to cook it.

But for the most important tool needed for a human to live a fulfilled life, the mind, there is no such manual. We don't have formal classes organized to teach how the mind works, our education curriculum does not apportion a segment for the teachings on the mastery of the mind, there are no structures put in place to allow every human understand the mind.

And this is not beneficial to anyone.

Every technology is a product of mind, and we understand everything through the thoughts and cogitations of the mind. All the great ideas every developed in the history of the world all took their roots in the mind, and they were all planted like seeds into the minds of other people.

If the mind has proven to be as useful in our history as humans, why then do we not understand it?

Harvard Professor, William James stated that "we humans use less than ten percent of our mind capacity". It should make you wonder what happened to the vast majority of our mind's capacity. Do they just go to waste, unearthed and unused? Oh yes, they do. And that is why humans are generally lazy in thought and action. The mind that should make us tick, and help us make decisions just lies fallow untapped. And when some provoking questions come to our minds, how many of us really attempt to search for answers? How many of us explore the limitless well of knowledge and possibilities we possess within our minds?

Another perspective to this striking statistic presented by the Professor is that, despite the great discoveries and giant strides humans have made since the beginning of the world, and through civilization, none of the geniuses and great men have used more than ten percent of their minds. Not Albert Einstein, not Leonardo da Vinci, not Aristotle, not Socrates, not Isaac Newton, not Michelangelo, not Wolfgang Amadeus Mozart, not even Galileo; no one, no human has ever used more than ten percent of the brain. Sit back, wonder, and think about that for a moment.

Humans have crossed the oceans, traveled into space, cured diseases, made weapons that can annihilate continents in minutes, developed artificial intelligence, mastered ether and waves, created beauty, explored the planets, transplanted body parts, defeated gravity, achieved extraordinary feats that were once unimaginable, yet, not even one single human has used more than ten percent of the mind.

As you would imagine, the human mind must therefore, be such a limitless seat of power and endless possibilities, and if you can master the mind, and find a way to explore its untapped resources and ability, then you can conquer the world, literally. And I hope that, as you read through this book, learn the wisdom it teachers, and put into practice the methods; you will acquire the key to unlock your mind and obtain its limitless possibilities.

This book is a user manual for your mind. It was written to show you how to become limitless and unstoppable and how you can set your mind free and allow it realise its full potential. The book will question some principles you have held on to throughout your lifetime, it will provoke some thoughts you have never considered, it might even make you doubt some of your beliefs, but I want to assure you that, when that happens, be rest assured that it is your mind turning over on itself, changing its course for better, and opening up new possibilities. And you are very much on your way to possessing and living life with a limitless mind and its countless benefits.

A limitless mind equips you to make life decisions that are sound, wise and long-lasting. It helps you conquer the restrictions within you that have been limiting you throughout your life. When your mind becomes limitless, you will have the ability to see things more clearly, approach matters more intelligently, and solve problems more efficiently.

With such wonderful rewards, don't you consider it absolutely necessary to possess such a powerful tool that unlocks all doors? Don't you want to have this invaluable ability to rule over your life and destiny? Do you want your mind to become limitless? What is stopping you?

Abstract

The first step to moving forward in life is always to identify and recognize the problems or challenges that had been holding one back all the while. And if you would seek to possess a limitless mind, you must first understand what has been hindering your mind from pushing the limits. What hinders the mind from being without boundaries? Why does your mind restrict itself to its limited ability? Or rather, why do you restrict your mind from achieving all that it can?

From my research, studies and experiences, I have been able to highlight and understand the following as impediments to a limitless mind. They are the agents that have been blocking you from getting the best out of your mind.

- Fear

- Limiting beliefs

- Self-doubt and Negative Self-talk

- Worry

- Procrastination

- Self-sabotage or Inner critic

- Weak Willpower

- Weak Self-image or Identity

- Comparison

- Instant Gratification or Pain

- Pleasure Principle

- Untrained Attention or Lack of Focus and Concentration

- Comfort Zone and Resistance to change

- Lack of Passion and Purpose

- Inability to Control Habits

- Control over Negative Emotions (jealousy, greed, anger, envy, guilt and regret)

I firmly believe that if I can help you solve each of the problems mentioned above, your life will take a new turn, your mind will become limitless and you will become unstoppable.

Let us now move forward, dive in, and discuss how to know, understand and master each of the aforesaid obstacles so that your mind can finally limitless as you become unstoppable.

Contents

Introduction   *v*

Abstract   *xi*

CHAPTER 1   From FEAR to FREEDOM   1

CHAPTER 2   Limiting Beliefs   43

CHAPTER 3   Proscrastination   77

CHAPTER 4   Self-Sabotage   91

CHAPTER 5   Self-Doubt and Negative Self-Talk   105

CHAPTER 6   Worry   113

CHAPTER 7   Comparison   121

CHAPTER 8   Instant Gratification   131

CHAPTER 9   Lack of Passion and Purpose   139

CHAPTER 10 Comfort Zone and Resistance to Change   147

CHAPTER 11 Self-Image/Identity   153

CHAPTER 12 Master The Power of Habit   159

CHAPTER 13 Attachment   165

CHAPTER 14 Paradigm, Emotions, Focus and Will-Power   171

CHAPTER
One

From FEAR to FREEDOM

(How to Master the Game of Fear)

Can you imagine how your life would be if you were free from all the fears that block your success and stop you from achieving your goal and prevent you from creating the life you desire? Have you ever wondered how comforting and good it would be if you could let of all your fears and live your life with absolute faith, confidence and strength? How would it feel if you can just be in total control of your life?

How would it feel if you can live your life full of confidence and certainty, without the constant fear of failure? How would it feel to free yourself from anxiety and getting nervous when you have to step up and make crucial decisions? Do you want to always be confident and be able to rise and act when it matters most?

This chapter has a potential to provide you with the breakthrough you would need. It is a ticket of your freedom from fear. If absorbed, understood, applied and practiced, I am sure the methods taught in this chapter are capable of handing you the important tool necessary to turn your dream life into reality.

This instructive story of a young man comes to mind.

This young man was living in his family home until his mother died. His father married another woman who had previously given birth to two children of different fathers. This new wife, the young man's stepmother, began to maltreat the young man, she cursed him every morning, and on one particular occasion, she even slapped him. The young man was nineteen at that time, and the only offence she accused him of was that he was asking for fees to apply for admission into the university. And that was the day the young man finally realized he must leave the house for his life to get better.

His father kicked against the decision, and even threatened to disown him and remove his name from the family register if he didn›t change his mind, but the young man never did. As he turned his back on the family, and walked away, his father rained curses on him; and one particular curse that stuck with the boy was when his father told him, so far he was the one whose reproductive cell birthed the young man, he would never succeed until he came back to the family. It was a very deep curse, and the young man winced when he heard his father make the pronouncement. But he didn't wave. He cried bitter tears as he left, but he never changed his mind. He had had enough, and he was resolute.

And so it was, this young man left the home he had known all his life, he left everything behind and moved in with one of the younger brothers of his mother who was living in the next town. He started taking odd jobs and joined his uncle to sell kitchen wares in the market. But on the cold nights, when he lay on the thick cloth he used as mattress, on the floor of the single room he shared with his uncle, his mind sometimes wander to the curse his father shouted at him.

He was finally able to pay the necessary fees for the entrance exams, but on the day of the exam, he couldn't forget the curse of his father; he kept it in his mind, and he became afraid he would fail. Well, it reflected in his results, as he barely passed the exam. But the average score he had was enough to give him admission into the university.

When he got into the school, he struggled throughout his stay, but once and again, he kept holding on to the curse of his father, and as his results became worse and worse each session. He was always living in fear of the curse of his father; and he attributed his failures to the evil pronouncements his father made when he left home.

When he was sent out of the school for his dismal academic performances, he didn't even cry; he convinced himself it was all due to his father's curse. He had spent three years in school, and he spent the years in fear of his father's curse, until he was kicked out. He joined his uncle in selling the kitchen wares, but he couldn't succeed still, just because of his fear and belief in the curse his father made.

On one of the hottest nights, when he was already twenty four, he was having a talk with his uncle outside the house when he began to narrate the bitter story of his life. He told him about the circumstances of his departure from home, and the curse of his father.

"My own father told me that so far he was the one who contributed to my conception and birth, I will never succeed in life until I return to him." The young man told his uncle, his voice broken and hopeless. "And that curse has proven to be true in my life till now."

He looked to his uncle, expecting him to look at him in pity and be sorrowful for him, but his uncle was smiling. His uncle shook his head and laughed.

"Oh! Didn't you know?" The uncle told the young man. "He is not your actual father. Your mother was already pregnant with you before he met him."

The young man couldn't believe his ears, and his uncle continued, "Your mother, my own immediate sister, told me all these before she died, and I always thought she would have told you."

"Don't tell me you believe the curse, and have been living all these years in fear of it." The uncle added.

The young man's mouth dropped open, and couldn't close for some moments as he realized he had been living in fear of something that was never real. He looked back at his uncle's face blankly and it dawned on his that he had been afraid of nothing for five good years.

He had wasted his life believing in a curse that was based on a nothing. He had constantly doubted his own ability just because he had allowed fear reign supreme in his life.

It was the next morning that this young man began a new phase of his life; he picked up himself, he dusted his past fear and failures aside, and he started living a new life of confidence and firm belief in his ability.

He reapplied to the same school he had been expelled from, and he applied for the same course. He scored thirty marks more than the average score he had before, and was always among the top ten best students of his class until he graduated.

The young man in this story finished school and started working in a private international company so popular I can bet you have heard of them in the news. Twenty years after he let go of his fears, this man is today, one of the most important decision makers in the company, and he has even written books on success.

So, where do you stand? Do you still want to continue living your life in fear? Or you want to put a stop to fear today, and start living a life of freedom. Where do you stand?

From my interactions with people who have found it hard to succeed, the number one thing that I have discovered stops people from achieving anything is FEAR. The most frequent factor that most successful people, if not all, have needed to overcome in the initial stage of their career is fear. And the one thing that has been limiting humans from getting the best out of life is fear.

It often serves as a mental cage without lock that you have put yourself into. Many people are stuck in a particular job or relationship they hate just because of fear, the fear of the unknown, the uncertainty and question of what if?

These people do not take necessary risks to get breakthrough in life, so they choose to continue living in a toxic environment, and keep bearing the in pain just because it familiar or predictable.

The first thing I would advise you, oh reader, is to brace yourself, make up your mind, gather all your strength, and Face your fear.

But what is Fear?

Once again, I will like to take one segment of definitions from the dictionary; this time from the Oxford Advanced Learners, which defines fear as "a bad feeling that you have when you are in danger, or when you feel that something bad might happen in the future."

I must emphasize that even from this uncomplicated academic description, it was pointed out that fear comes from a feeling that something might happen in the future. Is there a probability that this particular thing might actually happen? Yes. Is there also a chance that this thing might eventually not even happen? Of course, yes.

So, why do we fear?

And from my experiences and studies, I have discovered that the likelihood of something we fear happening is always higher than the probability of it not happening; but humans would rather believe the worst case scenario, even if it is just a one percent chance.

Psychologists also explain that Fear is an automatic emotional response to external or internal stimuli that is interpreted as threat or danger by the brain. It is an automatic response against threat or threatening situations, whether real or imaginary. Let me repeat the last phrase, "whether real or imaginary".

Fear is a default mechanism hardwired by your entire being, and designed to protect you. Fear, whether real or imaginary, kicks in when you find yourself in unfamiliar territories and face situations that are new to you. When you start getting afraid, understand that it is just your being, trying to protect your physical body or self-image.

Now that we know fear is a response to anything interpreted as danger, and that it comes as a form of protection, what are the things that cause us for?

Natural Triggers for Fear

- Unusual or unexpected sound: certain sounds have the ability to make us afraid just because we have associated those forms of sound to danger. This is what is often depicted in horror movies. Generally, sounds have a way of triggering our emotions; like the happiness we feel in comedy sounds, the love we feel in romantic sounds, or the sadness in the slow melancholic background music of dramas. Sounds can reach into our mind and manipulate it to become afraid.

- Vague visual stimuli or darkness: from our early years, we have learnt, either consciously or subconsciously, to become afraid of some images and fear at the sight of some things. And if we happen to tie these images to a bad memory, we may begin to feel fear every time those images are brought before our eyes.

- Sudden movement: There is often an automatic involuntary response humans feel when there is a sudden shift or movement around them, especially when they didn't expect it. The rush of adrenaline motivates the mind to prepare to fight or be in flight.

- Loneliness: The human mind always wants and even longs for the connection to other humans. Humans are social animals; we thrive in one another's company. This is why fear set in when people feel alone and lonely, without friends or partners. The empty void left in our heart cries out to be filled with conversations with other people and thoughts about other humans.

- Abandonment and loss: When we feel left behind, and abandoned or lost, we often feel a pang of helplessness in form of fear. Our minds anticipate the disconnection we would have from our family and friends. And as we seek to be joined back to our people, fear begins to enter our minds, just thinking about the possibility of losing them forever.

- Unfriendly faces: We generally grow accustomed to the people we have known and trusted. And when we see the trusted faces even in a crowd, we often smile as peace of mind automatically returns. But when we behold unfriendly or strange faces, we begin to consider dangerous possibilities that might happen; and fear also quickly set in as our minds imagine worse situations.

- Potential pain or discomfort: The promise of pain is enough to cause fear in our minds. When we look forward to some levels of discomfort, or pain, our mind begins to brace itself in anticipation of these negative feelings; and the way the mind does this is by initiating fear.

Unconscious triggers of fear also exist. Fear is relative in nature, and different people react differently according to images or audio stimuli interpretations and limiting beliefs. People who have very high survival instincts fret much more quickly than people who are lower on the survival scale.

Here is a list of some triggers: self-doubt, lack of confidence (mismanaged memory), lack of certainty, feeling of being undeserving (self-limiting beliefs), lack of worthiness, past experiences, lack of skill and know-how, untrue beliefs, self judgement, a painful memory, and imagination. All fears start with imagination- an anticipation of what is to come upon us; even before it comes. The wilder the imagination, the more afraid you become.

I must also point out that the idea of losing something, physical or psychological, is one of the most common ways to initiate fear.

You are born with three major fears. These fears come to you with instinct, and you can easily notice it in babies and very young children. A child may not fear something as dangerous as fire, but these three things will certainly make the child afraid.

- Fear of falling
- Fear of abandonment
- Fear of sounds

Mechanism of Fear

Through the scientific study of the brain, we have a glimpse of how the mind works when fear sets it, and you can now understand the anatomical and psychological changes that happen when you become afraid.

When you receive the stimulus in form threats or thoughts through any of your five senses, and your mind too, you undergo what is known as perception and interpretation. Immediately this happens, the amygdala, located deep in the brain's medial temporal lobe, becomes activated and responds to the stimulus by releasing the chemicals, adrenaline, the emergency hormone, and cortisol, a stress hormone. These two hormones work in concert and cause high heartbeat which results in the pumping of more blood into the muscles of the hands and legs. This is also accompanied by high breathing rate which provides more oxygen.

You should also understand that when this amygdala gets activated, it typically highjacks the neocortex, the frontal part of the brain that is responsible for logic and reasoning, and then shuts off the intellect. And this is the reason why you may make decisions that are not logically when you are afraid. Therefore, if you live in constant fear, through these biochemical processes I have already explained, you will never be able to make sound intellectual decisions about your life, or take the wisest course of action.

As I said earlier, Fear, whether real or imaginary, is generally a response your mind elicit when it is trying to protect your physical body or self-image from damage. And in order achieve your safety it generate three responses.

Three Kinds of responses to Fear

- Flight
- Fight
- Freeze

The three responses I have listed above are self-explanatory. It is either you run, you stand and defend yourself, or you just stay inactive, usually temporarily.

These three types of fears are also the three manners of life humans exhibit when they begin to have thoughts that make them afraid. Most folks run from the problem and quit. Some stand their ground and face the fear, fighting it and resisting the problem till it succumbs. And there are some humans too who don't act at all, when fear comes into their mind, they continue to live with it, without making any attempt to find a way out.

Which group do you think you are classified? Flight, fight, or freeze?

Types of Fear: Two types of Fear exist: Real Fear, and Imaginary Fear which can also be termed potential fear or irrational fear (phobias).

1. Real fears include fears of things that are very likely to happen, and in fact, might have happened in the past, whether to you personally or to someone you know. Examples of real fear include the fear of lions or snakes, fear of accidents and physical pain, fear of loss of money, health, friends, or knowledge (in the case of dementia). This type of fear quickly activates survival mode, and thus, is very useful and important for our survival. In fact, humans would have gone into extinction without this fear mechanism.

2. Imaginary fears are generally irrational fears that are built on the imagination, rather than reality. These imaginary fears include:

- Fear of failure: this is fear of not accomplishing or achieving a set target or goal, or succeeding in an activity. It is one of the most common fears associated with people of great minds.

- Fear of rejection: this fear comes during interaction with people, especially when you need people and begin to wonder if they would not refuse to accept or acknowledge you or your ability.

- Fear of judgement: it comes when you fear that people discover something about you, they may start making conclusions about you that might lead them to start treating you differently, or discriminating against you.

- Fear of success: it is a strange fear, but it is just as real. It is the fear you feel when you begin to get afraid that things are going too well for you, and you start doubting if you can handle the goodwill and weight of expectations that come with success.

- Fear of commitment: this fear comes long when you start considering binding or engaging yourself to a person or course of action. You begin to panic and ask yourself if you really want to make such bold decisions that might deprive you of other opportunities.

- Fear of shame or embarrassment: when you feel you have some sort of inadequacies, you may become afraid of it being exposed to the world or made public. This fear often results in decisions that are extreme as you try to protect your image.

- Fear of change: when you have grown so comfortable and familiar with a constant patter, or environment, the fear of changing into something new may begin to set it, as you fear that the unknown may not be as good as what you have now.

- Fear of disappointment: this is the fear that keeps people from trusting others. You start feeling that they will let you down, and your mind becomes filled with fear in a bid to protect yourself.

- Fear of poverty: this often has to do with your upbringing. When you feel that you might end up like your parents, or people in your community, who lived and died poor, fear sets in, as you grow older and become more wary of the problem of poverty.

- Fear of being wrong or looking foolish: this is the fear that makes you not want to attempt anything original, this fear has a way of killing creativity, as you become afraid of looking foolish if you end up being wrong.

- Fear of public speaking: this is also tied to the preceding fear. It is the feeling you get when you fear that things would go wrong anytime you think about facing people and saying your mind.

- Fear of being unloved: one of the most basic needs of every human is the need to feel loved; and when you are starved of this need for a long time, you might start to be afraid of losing it when you finally have it. This has destroyed a number of relationships as a partner starts to fear that the love give could be taken away.

- Fear of loneliness: since our mind has been conditioned to want association and companionship, it is not uncommon for people to fear the thoughts of being lonely.

- Fear of unknown: this is a fear common to every human since we have limited knowledge of time and events. And when we face a future unknown, fear kicks in as we begin tom ask the usual what ifs?

- Fear of being ignorant, being blamed, taking action and responsibility are all also similar to the fear of being wrong and being committed. You begin to fear that you would fail if you are trusted with some responsibility, and therefore take the blame for such failure.

- Phobias are also irrational fear. Different phobias have been listed and defined in the twenty first century alone. And these fears are as valid as the fear of death or fear of failure.

Causes of Imaginary Fear

One of the most common causes of fear is **Limiting Beliefs**. When you fill your head with a lot of strange and superstitious beliefs, your mind also begins to hold on firmly to such beliefs, leaving you with a fearful disposition when those things happen. Some folks believe that a broke mirror, crossing a black cat, or walking under a ladder are bad omens that provoke evil outcomes. And when you spend all your time thinking in this manner, you will end up living your life in fear. This is the same thing that happened to the young man in our story.

Anticipating the worst possible outcome is also one of the causes of fear. When you lay your hands on a task, begin a new journey, or start a new relationship, and even from the very beginning, you are already prepping yourself for failure and collapse, expecting things to go awry, then you will ultimately live in constant fear. A pessimist will always become defeated even before defeat comes, and fear will rule over the life of a person who expects bad results. This is why, when two persons are in an elevator, one of them starts to get afraid while the other is at perfect peace.

Fear is also caused by **Traumatic Past Experiences**. Since human memories linger for a very long time, and sometimes even a lifetime, especially when very bad events happen to us, it is very easy for the mind to become conditioned to fear any similar event. For example, a man who was attacked in an alley may never pass that alley for the rest of his life; and someone who witnessed the Mumbai attacks can live in constant fear of sound. This is how many phobias develop in the mind.

How Fear Block our Success and Motivation

Like I said before, having real fear is a good thing as it is very necessary for your survival. But imaginary fear only blocks you from achieving success. The imaginary fears that have already been mentioned above, like the fear of failure or fear of public speaking, all have a way of stopping you from getting the success that you deserve.

These fears will always cause you not to take up challenges, or make you hesitate when you should take your chances; and if you eventually find a way to start doing that what you want, the fears will make you to start giving excuses, procrastinating, worrying, doubting yourself, and generally failing at the end of the day.

This is why I consider fear as one of the foremost self-defeating behaviours; as we will discuss in detail in the coming chapters.

Someone aptly explained fear when by saying, "*Fear is faith for the things you don't want.*" I will repeat that more plainly for emphasis; Fear is actually a strong faith that things you don't want will come to you. And this is the exact way fear actually operates. It causes the release of the things we fear.

Consider the beasts in the fields, the fearsome tigers and lions. It is quite interesting that even they understand how fear works. They can discern fear and react to it. When they sense that you are afraid of them, they grow more confident. Animals that are predatory can immediately sense fear, and it arouses in them the aggression to catch their prey.

Most of us have witnessed how a person who has a fear of dogs always seems to arouse a desire in even the most docile dog pets to attack him. This is the very thing that the enemy does to us spiritually. Fear arouses demonic forces to swarm to the vulnerable. Likewise, faith repels them.

This is why in different parts of the world, tribes exist which can walk on hot coals of fire with calmness, or tame wild animals; the only difference between the men and women of such tribes and you is simple. While you fear, they have faith.

Fear always kills motivation. And in fact, the strongest of motivations can crumble in the face of the smallest fear. Once fear begins to whisper in your mind, your motivation starts to fizzle away until you lose it all.

Motivation → Fear → Excuse or Blame →
Procrastination → Failure

This simple flow diagram above shows the steps that fear uses to deprive you of success.

You feel motivated when you set a goal but with time, motivation reduces and you fall short of achieving your goals. Even without fear, a human's mind loses motivation, but when fear is now thrown into the equation, the motivation dies quicker.

Typically, when you set a goal and think about the outcome, it activates the left frontal cortex of your brain, which then activates your motivation and results in a burst of energy, excitement, joy, passion, action and confidence.

But after some time has passed, and you start activating imaginary fear, the fear circuit replaces motivation, and negative thought and past memories begin to come into your mind. Automatically, your right frontal lobe takes those negative thoughts and projects them into the future. Hence, you start to anticipate negative outcomes- which shuts down the motivation circuit and activates the three kinds of fear responses we discussed earlier.

- Flight response comes in form of self-doubt, insecurity, procrastination, and low confidence.

- Fight response comes through blame, complaint, justification, excuses, and rationalization of why you cannot work, or achieve your goal.

- Freeze is observed as inaction, only wishful thinking not backed by action, feeling of being overwhelmed, confusion, and absolutely giving up.

Steps or Methods to Overcome Fear

It is important for me to tell you that you cannot absolutely eliminate fear. But you definitely can apply effective strategies that can help deal with it so that you can change the way you see fear.

1. **Take Action**: action cures fear in the same way inaction helps it grow. Therefore, the longer an action is postponed, the more the fear and anxiety.

'*Jisse darlage kardlo*', meaning, '*act on the things you fear*' in English, is an expression that will always remain true. When there is a fear in your mind, the best thing to do is to act on it, to take the decision to do that exact thing you fear, and test the fear.

This is why an important condition to consider before taking action is to first ask yourself whether your fear is real or imaginary.

As I already told you, real fear is good for you. Therefore, you should not apply this method if fear is real. You may not take direct actions if you have valid real fears. For example, it may not be considered wise for you to jump off the roof of a building just because you want to face your fear of heights and take action. You also cannot go to the nearest zoo in your city, and go into the lion's cage because you want to overcome your fear of lions. This is not what I am teaching. No.

Hence, it is very important to first identify if your fear is imaginary. Then you must also evaluate if there is any risk of causing physical harm to yourself or other people before you act on your fear. If there is no physical harm to anyone, it is only then you can act on your fear. If your fear is the fear of public speaking, you have to understand that this fear is just an imaginary fear. There is really nothing to fear. The public will not gather and beat you. Literally, nothing will happen, no physical harm to you or the audience listening, so let the fear go. Take action, climb the podium and speak.

This truth is illustrated in the story of a man who was walking towards a temple and while he was in the way, he saw two dangerous bulldogs that were tied to a chain. Still, this man got frightened and started thinking and asking himself what if the dogs unchained themselves and attack him. He kept walking, but every few seconds he would look back to ensure the dogs were still tied to a chain. He looked back five more times and when he was looking back the sixth time, he saw those dogs getting untied and running dangerously toward him. He got very frightened at first, but then he started running towards dogs instead of running away from them. This act shocked and frightened the dogs and they got afraid and ran away.

It is a universal truth; facing your fears or problems is an effective way to eliminate them.

2. **Self-talk and Asking Right Questions**: our subconscious mind provides answers to the questions we ask consciously. If we ask weak and negative questions, our mind will also start to supply negative answers. For example, if you ask 'What if I fail?', your mind will supply you with answers, telling you the different things that can go wrong. If you ask 'Can I do it?', your mind will give you a thousand reasons why you cannot do it. A woman that asks, 'Won't I die?' will get answers from his mind, explaining why she would die. And a man that always wonders, 'Will this good thing last?', will get responses from his mind, telling him everything that can go wrong to cut short his joy. The questions you ask yourself subconsciously is vital in determining your predominating thoughts; and this in turn, determines if fear will rule over your life.

Conversely, if you form the habit of always allowing the right questions go through your mind, and make sure it is only good thoughts and expectations that you look forward to, your mind will become subconsciously conditioned to let go of your fears and give you strength to forge ahead. If you ask 'What if I get success?', your mind will supply only positive outcomes as examples. If you ask yourself, "How will I become rich?", your mind will supply answers that would show you what you need to do to become rich. It is just how the mind works. It looks for answers to questions it is asked. It is like the Newton's third law of motion- "Actions and reactions are equal and opposite in direction." I mean, it is what you question your mind that it answers; and this answer will be in equal weight and substance with the question asked. A man who was diagnosed with cancer was told by the doctor that he had less than a year to live. He asked, 'A year, or just over a year?' Note that the doctor told him less than a year. But while you and I might have asked, 'How many months", reducing the number of days, he asked if he had more than a year. And I must tell you, this man lived for fourteen months before he eventually died. He added extra months to his time in the world just because he asked the right question.

Do you feel your mind with positive thoughts and questions? Or you think defeated thoughts. Well, look no further for the cause of your failure; they are right there in your mind and the prevailing thoughts and questions. One sure way to kill your fear is to always fill your mind with reasons why things will end up positively.

3. **Turn your Fear into Fuel**: You can, and must, learn to use your fear to power up your mind until the fear turns into a fuel that helps you complete tasks, and do what you must. One of the ways to do this is through the Power of Negative Consequence. You can imagine the consequences of not doing a task when fear of doing it is stopping you. And in this way, you can use your fear as a fuel.

For example, an average-looking guy was afraid of telling a hot girl in his gym that he loved her. He was thinking that he was not smart, hot and good looking enough for her. He also told himself that since he was not from a rich background, this girl would reject him and she might embarrass him. Here, the fear of rejection, and the fear of not being smart enough have kicked in him, and dissuaded him.

So, how can he use his fear as a fuel? He can do this if he starts thinking about the negative consequences of not telling that girl about his feeling. I mean, he might begin to reconsider what would happen if he holds back his feeling. She will never know his feeling, and someone else may approach her before he does, and he stands the risk of losing her forever. Therefore, this fear of losing the girl of his dream forever can serve as a fuel to power him and give him the courage he needs to walk up to the girl and tell her how he feels. Thus, the consequence of not doing something has turned his fear into fuel.

You are afraid of showing people your true self, and what you can do? Think, instead, of what would happen if you continue to pretend and hide. Your peculiarity will die with you, and your ability will go to waste. Do you want that? Do you want to die without having lived as truly as possible?

You fear failure? Think about what would happen if you don't make an attempt. You will continue to be overlooked, underestimated and disrespected. Are these not enough reasons to try and see if you would fail or succeed? If you fail, at least, you can be proud of yourself and know what to correct and improve on.

4. **Power of Acceptance**: This simply means that you imagine the worst possible outcome that can happen when you take an action, accept the outcome and do what you want to do anyway. And I can personally assure you that this works like a magic trick. When you imagine the worst and accept it, then the intensity of worry, fear and stress reduces and you can act more confidently.

For example, while doing skydiving there is a constant fear you feel that tells you that things might go wrong. But the moment you accept the fear, and tell yourself that even if things go wrong, it will still be a part of the adventure, the fear leaves immediately.

If you want to take an examination, and your mind begins to whisper to you that you would fail, smile and reply the fear by telling yourself that even if you fail, you will take the examination again. You like someone but you are afraid of being rejected, ask yourself, what is the worst thing that could happen? Accept the outcome and do what you want to do.

The first time I had to speak to a large crowd, my heart was beating wildly some moments before my name was called, fear enveloped my mind and I was tempted to run. But I used this simple trick and it worked perfectly. I imagined the worst thing that could happen; that the audience might hate the sight of me, and boo me off. I smiled and told myself it would be a funny story to tell my friends even if it happened. And then, I heard my name called, stood up and walked up to the podium. As I spoke the first words, I listened for the boos to start, but they never did. I smiled and continued to talk. When I finished speaking, the applause was almost deafening.

It is this same method I am recommending to you. Accept the worst possible outcome, and do what you want to do nonetheless.

5. **The 4R Technique**: This is a method designed by John Assaraf outlining the steps to overcoming fear.

The first step is to **Recognize** your fear. You must become aware of the fear you are feeling. Identify it, accept that you are feeling it, and note the exact thing that makes you afraid.

Release your fear: think about the fear you are facing, inhale deeply through your nose and exhale from your mouth while thinking the fear is moving out of your system, and completely leaving your body. Do this with intent and repeat the process until you can actually feel the feel the fear dissipating from you.

Reframe: give your fear situation a new meaning or context. There are different kinds of reframing techniques in the neurolinguistic programming (NLP). For example, the fear of failure can be handled by reframing your meaning of failure. You can choose to consider failure as a feedback and opportunity to learn and improve.

In this light, though people say Thomas Edison failed more than a thousand times before he invented the light bulb, you can choose not to consider it as failure, and instead, look at it in another perspective. Thomas Edison certainly didn't think that he failed all those times when he said he had successfully invented a thousand ways of not building an electric bulb.

The types of reframing include belief reframing, meaning reframing, and context reframing. Robert Kiyosaki also said 'either we win or we learn'. And certainly, Kiyosaki would know what success really means.

Other words of wisdom that you may find useful as you redefine Failure include:

'Faster you fail, faster you learn and faster you grow.'

'If you want to increase the rate of success, increase the rate of failure.'

'The presence of a shadow is an evidence of the presence of light"

And similarly, I would like to add that 'The possibility of failure is a concrete evidence of the possibility of success.'

Write down these quotes, place them in a strategic part of your room, and read it to yourself every morning.

Retrain: Affirmation and visualization are two of the best methods of training. You affirm that your courage, strength and faith, and tell yourself that you are better off without fear. You let go of the fear and doubts while speaking to your mind about your new decisions. You tell yourself that fear has lost its hold over your life, and speak against its existence. Whenever you have negative thought that can create fear, you speak words of affirmation that are helpful in overcoming fear. Delete the words of fear being spoken to your mind and infuse the opposite positive thought by saying it three times.

For example, when fear speaks to you and tells you that you are not smart enough to achieve your goal, talk back against it and say, 'Cancel, Cancel, Delete, Delete!' Then speak the positive words of affirmation to yourself, 'I have all power to achieve my goals, I have all power to achieve my goals, I have all power to achieve my goals!'

Tell yourself again and again, 'I will succeed!', 'I can do it!' Repeat these words three times whenever fear comes to your mind.

The Visualization technique to overcome fear is done by imagining yourself overcoming the fear and celebrating your win over fear. The hot air balloon Visualization technique is recommended for those who really want to overcome their fear.

Steps for the hot air balloon visualization technique:

Sit in a comfortable position and relax.

Inhale deeply and slowly exhale through your mouth.

Repeat for five breaths.

Imagine that you are standing in a beautiful garden and there is a hot air balloon which is hooked to a rope on ground. Move close to the balloon and imagine your biggest fear; it can be fear of failure, fear of public speaking, fear of what others think of you, or fear of being judged and criticized. Allow yourself feel that fear. Try to locate where exactly you are feeling this fear. It may be in your heart, head, stomach, hand or even your feet. Focus on where you have pinpointed this source of this fear. If you can't exactly locate the source of fear, or feel the fear in your entire body, then choose your heart. Once the source location of feeling is established, give that feeling on the location a colour; any colour that comes to your mind. Now, imagine that the colorful feeling is rising from the source and leaving the location in a powdered form. And then imagine that this lifted coloured fear is getting dumped in the hot air balloon.

Repeat same process for other fears as well.

Once you have dumped all your fears in the depth of the hot air balloon, imagine that you cut the ropes that were keeping the balloon hooked to the ground.

As you cut the rope, the balloon starts to fly higher and higher until it quickly disappears into the clouds.

This is a very power visualization to overcome fear. Do it with relax body and mind. I assure you that you will feel amazing, happy, confident and lighter after doing it.

This same method has been prescribed for many people, and it has worked for them. So, have no doubt that it will work for you.

5. **Build your Confidence**- the Maasai tribe of Tanzania are popular for hunting male lions. In this practice of show

of courage and strength, it is not uncommon for some of them to lose their lives or get injured. But do you know why they still continue to hunt these fearsome beasts? It is because they have so much confidence in themselves and their abilities. And this type of confidence is the one that remains strong and unshaken even when one of them is fatally wounded by a lion. This confidence has completely driven out fear from their minds, leaving them with a special kind of powerful belief in themselves.

Through my studies into human psychology, I have been able to outline the five most effective ways to build confidence.

i. Use positive affirmations and say good things about yourself that bring good feelings.

ii. Identify what you are good at, and make it a point to do this thing as often as you can.

iii. Learn how to accept compliments and praise for what you do.

iv. Don't criticize yourself up to the point where you start thinking of quitting. You can assess yourself as often as you want, and be sincere with your assessment, but when you note the places where you must improve, don't beat yourself up too much.

v. Remind yourself of your true worth, and never sell yourself cheap. Know, with utmost certainty, how special you are and place a high value on yourself.

Once your confidence level is high and you trust yourself well enough, fear will die out of your life.

Applications of the 4R Technique in Overcoming the some of the most Common Fears

Fear of failure

You can recognize the fear of failure easily by observing how your mind reacts to tasks given to you. Do you look forward to doing the tasks and taking the step, or you start fretting just thinking about the actions to be taken? If you find yourself worrying about the outcome of a task even before you take the first step, then, you have a fear of failure. And once you start giving yourself excuses why you may not be able to do a thing which you have never tried, that is a clear indication that you have a fear of failure.

Once you identify the fear, you can then release the fear from your body. Inhale deeply from your nose and exhale from our mouth while thinking the fear is moving out of your system. Visualize yourself letting go of the fear of failure, and being totally free of it.

Then, you must reframe this fear of failure by understanding that many of the people who are successful today have failed more number of times than you. Think about the number of times the great Michal Jordan had to fail before he could become so good at basketball. Even world changers like Abraham Lincoln failed in his attempt to become the President of the United States multiple times. Convince yourself that if Thomas Edison, Elon Musk , Sachin Tendulkar, A.P.J Kalam, Stephen Hawkings and the first men to fly, The Wright Brothers, if these great men could fail, you are no exception; you can fail too. It is alright to fear, therefore, it is needless to fear failure since you can see from the life of these great accomplishers that Failure is nothing but a very good teacher.

The Achievement Cycle goes like this, Do → Fail → Learn → Improve → Do Again → Fail → Learn → Improve → Keep trying till you succeed.

Do you remember how many times you failed before you could write the alphabet 'A' without the teacher's guiding hand? Do you know how many times you fell before taking your first step to walk? How many times did you fall before learning to ride the bicycle? So, why fear failure now when everything you have learnt in this life has been done after much failure?

Mahatma Gandhi went to prison more than ten times, and failed to win people to his ideology for more than ten years before he was eventually recognized and began having followers who believed him. Did Gandhi give up all those times? No, he didn't. So, why would you? Why will you be as afraid of failure as to give up before you succeed?

When you have reframed your mind successfully, it will become quite easy to Retrain your mind by affirming your freedom from the fear of failure and visualize yourself overcoming this fear of failure. Follow the hot air balloon visualization technique as I described earlier, and let out all your fear.

Fear of judgement

You will be able to Recognize that you have this fear if you find yourself always hesitating before speaking your mind, asking questions or giving opinions. You can be in a meeting, conference or on a date, and though everyone is speaking freely, you still hold back and just smile along despite having something on your mind. You have the fear of being judged if you are the type of person who goes out of his or her way to pretend that he has no problem or challenges.

Once you recognize this problem and identify this fear, you can then work on releasing this fear out of your body system by following the processes and steps I have already explained. Inhale and exhale until you push out the fear of being judged out of you.

When you can feel the fear leaving your body, and you start to feel free, you can move to the next step and reframe your mind by looking at things from a new perspective. As yourself, if people find out your shortcomings, what would they do? Are there really people without weaknesses and limitations? Is there anyone in the entire world who has a perfect knowledge of every single thing in life? So, why will you be afraid of being judged and condemned just because you are not right, or just because the people find you unusual?

Besides, why are you too bothered about what other people might think of you? Do they have any power over you except the one your fear has given them?

The fear of being judged is one of the most limiting fears as it will not allow you express yourself freely and share your views. And if you make a habit of never expressing yourself, you will not do anything of substance in your lifetime. So many wonderful ideas have been crushed for the sole reason that the originator of such idea has the fear of being wrong and judged.

Many people do not pursue their dreams and passion just because they are afraid of what other people think about them. Some persons also miss out on love and relationship because the fear of being seen with their partners and judged by other people. The simple solution to this fear is for you to be determined to stop being a people pleaser.

You cannot give people power over your life. I will repeat that for emphasis; do not give people power over your life. Care about people but don't care what they think about you. Set yourself free of this fear and limitation. These people are judging you on the basis of their perception, ability, attitude, knowledge, ignorance and attitudes. Therefore, what they think about you cannot tell the truth about you; hence, it is not your reality.

Why do humans have the fear of judgement? Why are you always afraid of getting things wrong? And why do you fear the thoughts people that are unrelated to you have about you? You must accept the reality that people will always make judgements about you. We live in the world of social media today where everyone and anyone can form their own opinion about you, and hold on to it, no matter how biased those opinions are.

People will judge the way you dress, look, walk, talk, behave so that they can feel superior to you, and feel more secured about them.

Having successfully reframed your mind and accepted that judgement will always be handed to you no matter what you do, you can then move to the next step of retraining your mind. First of all, affirm that your fear is baseless and pointless. Convince yourself that the opinions of other people do not really matter to you, and should therefore, not affect you in the slightest bit. Speak out this new belief you have acquired and tell yourself as loud as you can, that fear is gone out of you.

Visualize yourself letting go of the fear of being judged with the hot air balloon and let the fear drift away into non-existence.

The fear of criticism, fear of public speaking, and the fear of being not smart enough are all in the same territory with the fear of being judged, and the same steps are taken to conquer the fears.

Since I believe you now know how to release and retrain your mind, I will briefly teach you how you can recognize the fear of rejection and the fear of the unknown, and I will also show you can reframe your mind to conquer these fears.

Fear of Rejection and Disappointment

You can recognize this fear by examining the way you respond to opportunities. When you have a chance to start a new relationship, do you become afraid at being turned down? When you apply for a position or opportunity, do you get panic or start having anxiety attacks just at the thought of people telling you 'No'? If your answer to any of these questions is yes, then you must accept that you have a fear of rejection.

The fear of rejection is a normal reaction of the mind when it wants to prepare you mentally and wants you to protect yourself from the rejection when it eventually comes.

So, how can you reframe your mind to understand and face this fear in order to be free of it? The solution is in the following words: Things will not always go your way.

I want you to note that, and believe it. Throughout history, people who have lived before us have all suffered some level of rejection at one time of their life or the other. And of a truth, the fact that you have been rejected does not directly translate to the fact that you are not good enough.

Sometimes, we are rejected despite doing our best. And that is where the consolation lies. If you have done your best, and presented the best version of yourself, you should not be too afraid of being rejected. If you have given one hundred percent of your effort and ability, you should not fear being disappointed and turned down. That can only mean that it is not the right time for you to have that thing, or you are not the best fit for the opportunity.

I have made several applications in my lifetime. I applied for scholarships when I was young, and I was rejected by most of them, I have applied for jobs in the past that I was rejected and came out disappointed. But do I have to start being afraid of rejections? No, because I have been accepted some few times too. And I want to believe that you too have recorded some form of success in the past.

You must understand that a missed opportunity or a rejection handed out to you today is nothing but a rehearsal and stepping stone for another opportunity tomorrow, which, in my experience, often turn out to be more beneficial and rewarding.

Hence, like all other imaginary fears, it is pointless to fear rejection or disappointment. It changes nothing. I heard a funny expression somewhere some years ago. It says, 'A man who cannot tell his heart to a woman because of fear of being rejected will end up arranging the chairs and preparing the venue on the day she marries; and his fear would finally leave him when it was too late.'

Don't be like this man who didn't do anything for fear of being rejected, your fear might leave you when the opportunity passes, never to return again.

Fear of the Unknown

In my studies, I have found out that this fear is present in almost all humans, though in different proportions. But while some have learnt to relish this fear, and turn it into a source of strength, many others have allowed this fear overcome them and beat them into inactivity.

I believe it is fairly easy to recognize this fear. We were born with it. It has been our companion since your mind came alive, showing up in questions like, 'What will I become?' 'How will tomorrow look like?' 'What does the future hold for me?' 'After now, what next?"

Like I said before, it is not necessarily a bad thing to feel this fear in very little measures; but when your fear now becomes so mighty that you begin to worry and hesitate to enjoy the present or even move into the future, it means this fear must be conquered.

The greatest men that ever walked the earth all had a fear of the unknown, they had some moments were they wondered about the future, and fear that the worst would happen. But you know what set them apart? It is the ability to put the fear aside, use it as a source of strength, and go out bravely into the unknown future with faith and courage.

Courage, someone said, is not the absent of fear; it is the strength to take a step forward despite fear. I will like you to read that again and internalize it until your mind is reframed.

Things that will happen will not stop just because you are afraid of them. And your fear of the unknown cannot change a single thing.

I will end this chapter with this poem I really love. I will like you to read it with conviction and ponder on the words as long as you can. It is a work of art that speaks volume about the needlessness of fear.

Should I stand or sit?

Should I lie or kneel?

If I stand, will the arrows get me?

If I sit, will the stones not crush me?

If I kneel, they will say I surrendered.

If I lie down, they'll say I am defeated.

How long will my heart wonder?

How long will I fear what is not?

Is this fear my only friend?

Or it is just a constant enemy.

Maybe there is nothing to fear.

Maybe I am afraid for nothing.

The only thing to fear is fear.

If I die or live, let me be.

The only thing to fear is fear.

CHAPTER
Two

Limiting Beliefs

"The only reason you don't have what you want is because of the story you keep telling yourself why you can't."

—Tony Robbins

Have you heard the expression, 'Your life is in your hands'? If you have heard it before, have you really thought about its meaning? Well, let me rephrase it by saying, 'Your life is in your mind.' When your mind is filled with beliefs that limit your growth and development, you cannot expect things to go far in life.

Belief is explained as an idea in which some confidence is placed. It is as simple as the definition suggests. All what thoughts of your life do you place your faith and confidence? What do you believe and live for? On which ideas do you hang your life? What do you believe?

The candid answers to these questions will go a long way in determining the decisions you will make daily, and you must know that it is the accumulation of decisions that make up your destiny.

Consider the case of the goldfish. Do you know that if you move a goldfish from a small fishbowl in your home and take it to a lake, the fish will continue to swim in the same small circle? Why will this happen? Because the goldfish has accepted the belief that if he swims farther, it is going to bump his nose. He has always believed that since it was just a kid, and that same belief has held true till it became an adult. The goldfish has always swum in a small circle; therefore, it believes that any other way is **"IMPOSSIBLE"**. And that is the thing with beliefs, we hardly ever change them.

However, when you learn to question your beliefs, you also question your limitations. And if your beliefs are true and helpful, they will withstand the scrutiny. But if they don't survive the questioning, maybe it is time for you to drop them and replace them with beliefs that can serve you better.

For instance, if you have the belief that you need money to make money, it will be a quite hard for you to succeed in a recession. If you believe you must always borrow to have money, you will never get out of debt throughout your lifetime. And if you believe that there are too many obstacles in your way to succeed, you will fail. It is what it is.

Like the goldfish that has been freed to swim in the lake, once you still think you are limited, you will never see the opportunities open wide before you. And your limitation is set by your beliefs.

Jack had lived all his life in the farmhouse his grandparents owned and passed down to his father. The width of the farm was the entire world he knew. And he didn't really ask for more than that. He thought life and fulfillment were all in the rearing of the cattle and growing of crops. And he learnt the family trade as soon as he could stand. Other than the writing, reading and some arithmetic he could do, he wasn't educated in the ways kids his age in other parts of the country were. The only thing he could do very well on a sheet of paper was to draw landscapes- and he was very good at it. Though his father always told him not to waste his time 'playing with colours like a kid', and 'grow up and work hard on the farms', at every chance he got, Jack drew on a large drawing book his mother got him.

In 1938, when he was eleven, a businessman came to the farm in a shiny car and the man brought his boy along with him. While the adults did business and signed contracts, Jack and the city boy also got talking. Jack showed him all the tricks he could play with the grasses and the cows. He also took the boy to the poultry and taught him how to make the hens sing. The two boys had a nice time for more than two hours as Jack showed the boy all the drawings he had made in his book.

And then, as the two of them walked across a field of corn, the city boy looked at Jack and asked him a question his classroom teacher had asked him and his classmates two years ago.

'What do you want to become in the future?' the city boy asked Jack.

Jack thought the question strange. He had never heard the question spoken before. And he didn't know how to answer. Though he understood what the boy asked, he didn't know he could be asked.

He didn't know he had a say in his life. All his life, the one thing he had known and been brought up with was the running of the farm. And since he was the first son of his father, he knew he would inherit the farmland when his father died; the same way his father had inherited the land from his own father.

Jack looked up and stared back at the city boy. 'Of course, I will own all this land and be the master.' He said cheerfully.

'What about the drawings? Don't you want to become painter or artist? The city boy asked.

Jack held his belly and started to laugh out very loudly. His fits of laughter went on for ten seconds before he controlled himself enough to look at the boy and see his face looking back at him doubtfully.

'That's a good joke,' Jack said, 'Come on, laugh. You are very funny.'

But the city boy didn't smile. He looked back at Jack and realized why Jack was laughing so hard. Jack didn't know it was possible to take drawing and painting as a career. No one has ever told Jack.

Soon afterwards, the fathers came for their boys and Jack said his goodbyes hurriedly. And the two boys never saw each other again.

Ten years later, a wave of diseases went through the country, and Jack's family lost half of their lands. They soon found themselves in debt, and were forced to see the other half.

Another five years later, Jack's father died. Jack was left fatherless at 26 years of age without the inheritance he had hinged his life on.

He left the farm and joined the crew working with the railway corporation. All he had learnt to use was his muscles and body, and he used it well. He worked his young life away at the railway and spent his nights thinking back at the days when he would run around the fields, happy and free.

Two or three times in a year, his mind would drift back to the city boy he had met on the farm, and he would wonder where the boy was. The question the boy asked would come back to him, but fifteen years later, Jack still laughed at the ridiculousness of the question.

He still hadn't learnt that drawing and painting were things he could do to make more. His beliefs, the ones place in his mind by the limited knowledge of his father, were still strong upon his mind.

He had no time to draw again, but he still had his drawing book with him. For some strange reasons, he held on to the book through the years; a memorial of the good days in the fields.

Jack was at the railway station one afternoon when he saw a man walking up to him. Though he knew they could be age mates, the man looked too sophisticated, so Jack removed his hat and bowed slightly. But the man stopped just in front of him, smiled and called cheerfully, 'Jack ol' boy!'

When Jack looked more closely at him, he realized it at once. It was the city boy. But he was no longer a boy. In his black suit and shiny shoes, he looked like a man who has seen the world.

The two young men found a space in a nearby cafe and talked. He told Jack about all his travels and how he had set up a servicing company in his own name. But when he asked Jack about his life, the tragic story Jack narrated made his eyes moist.

'Do you still draw?' He asked Jack. And Jack shook his head and said 'No.'

'Can you still draw?' He asked again. Jack nodded and murmured a feeble 'Yes.'

'I told you before, Jack. Your drawings and paintings are good enough to be considered a career.'

Like he did decades ago, Jack laughed again, though this time in a more subdued manner.

'You don't believe me, do you?' The company man asked Jack.

Jack looked back at him with unbelieving eyes. He was starting to suspect the man was trying to play a fast one on him. He eyes him suspiciously, and wondered what he had that the company man could steal.

'Do you still have that drawing book where you painted the landscapes and the birds?' He asked Jack.

Jack handed him the book and he promised Jack he would be back in another month. The man went back into the city with the book.

When he returned, he returned the drawing book to Jack with some pages pulled out. Jack frowned when he noticed that some pages were missing, but before he could protest, the man handed him an envelope and smiled.

Jack eyed the envelope and opened it slowly. Bills of cash were inside it. When he counted, the money inside the envelope was exactly the same as his earning for a month.

Jack could barely contain himself. He drew the company man to a shade and asked him to tell him everything.

'Jack ol' boy!' the man said in his cheerful manner. 'I told you, didn't I? But you didn't believe me. I told you your drawings and paintings could fetch you money. I sold some of the pages in your book and a collector of art bought them all. I could have sold more, but he said he would buy until he saw the artist who made them all.'

And so, in the summer of 1955, Jack followed Edward, the company man back into the city. He had nothing except the money he made from the drawings already sold, but even as he stepped into the train that led into the city, Jack felt something crushing away from his mind.

It was the belief that had limited him for almost two decades; the same belief that had held him back from achieving anything worthwhile even though his talent was always with him.

And as Jack looked out the window and saw the trees running backwards, he felt a little regret at the time he had wasted just because he believed Art wasn't a career.

J & E Painting and Publishing, the company of the two young men set up two years after they arrived into the city lived on long after they died.

What do you believe? Where do you stand? What drives you? Which principles about life do you hold on to? And how productive have been those beliefs? I ask again, what do you believe?

What is Belief?

The dictionary defined Belief as a strong feeling that something exists, or is true; a strong feeling that something is true. What is your own truth?

Jack in the preceding story has his truth passed down to him by his father, and he believed it firmly. He never doubted it, because he felt, no, he knew; that that his father was right, and no one can get riches from making paintings on a piece of paper. This fact of his was true to him, and existed, even if it was only in his mind, and that of his father.

What is your own fact? In most cases, beliefs are not explained or based on evidence or proof. They are just tenets that we have accepted to be true and we live our lives with the firm conviction that they are true.

The Power of Belief

Our beliefs dictate our subconscious thoughts and the decisions we take based on these thoughts. Your belief can either work for you negatively or positively; but without doubt, it has the power to shift your path in life.

A man who believes there is no life without academic qualifications will spend all his life gathering as much certificates as he could. On the other hand, a man who has been taught early in life that education can come from within the walls of a school, or outside the school, would live with much more freedom since he knows he can still get some learning through other means.

And this simple belief adopted by both the academic man, and the worldly man, is powerful enough to dictate their decisions, choices or successes. In fact, it can determine their life.

Once the academic man doesn't get his hands on the certificates he so desires, he would automatically believe he has failed, and this truth of his will be reflected in the other parts of his life, and the way he relates with others. Conversely, if the academic man acquires all the certificates he wants, he will be happy, and at peace with the world because his own belief and definition of achievement and success has been fulfilled.

But what about the man of the world? In the first place, once he tries to acquire an academic qualification and fails on the first attempt, it is almost certain he would seek for knowledge elsewhere, since he has been convinced that he can get education from any part of life. Besides, even if he gets the certificates, he would not be as fulfilled as the academic man; he would still continue seeking for other forms of education.

And since fulfillment determines your happiness, it is important to define what makes you fulfilled, and you can only do that by redefining your beliefs.

The power of belief hasn't been as illustrated as the story of the woman who was admitted into the hospital and insisted that she must be given intravenous fluid. The doctors looked at her charts, diagnosed her, and advised her to sleep for a while, use some prescription drugs and observe her response for three days. But just as the doctors were speaking between themselves, the woman kept telling the nurse nearest to her that she must be given the fluid.

When the nurse told the doctors, they disagreed and refused. They went ahead with their own assessments, but three days later, the woman's situation had worsened. The doctors came around and compared charts again but they got confused.

When the doctors left, the nurse obliged the woman and fixed the IV fluid into her body. It took only twelve hours for this woman to recover her health, and become strong enough to be discharged the next day.

When she was asked, the nurse told the doctors that nothing was in the fluid besides saline solution and they quickly understood that it was her own belief that worked on her psychologically, and blocked the palliating effects of the drugs. And it was still her belief that empowered the IV fluid and made it work for her.

And this is one thing I want you to understand and internalize. Your belief, no matter how strange or common, has the power to either work for you positively or negatively.

Once you understand this, you will begin to sift through people's teachings and opinions, and become more careful about the beliefs you accept and the ones you reject.

Types of Belief

Existence: This is one of the simplest beliefs. It is the belief that something actually exists and is present in a space in time. That is, whether tangible or intangible, such entity is in existence. The most common of this kind of belief is the belief in God, the Devil, spirits, the soul, the afterlife, and goodness or evil nature of humans. These beliefs are often very strong in the mind, and very powerful too as they typically guide what you feel is right or wrong.

Causation: this type of beliefs seeks to explain how the world works, as humans try to determine causes and effects. The law of karma that suggests that a man reaps what he sows is one type of such beliefs. We try to find a correlation between one event and another event using this belief. Since the human mind always wonders why something happens, we start to believe in reasons and causes.

Perception: This type of belief is based on any or all of our five senses; what we hear, see, speak, taste, understand or feel. They are beliefs that are based on actual evidence or even scientific research. The rules that guide our health and the laws of physics are all based on our perceptions. It is a general belief that whatever we throw up will drop back down due to gravity, and we can actually demonstrate this belief on our own to verify its validity.

Opinions: These are our personal interpretations of the observations and judgements we have made though our lifetime. Sometimes, opinions can be transferred from one person to another through teaching, and once this opinion becomes strongly held by our mind, it translates into a belief. The rules of commonsense and the societal cultures are opinions that have been adopted by the majority, and therefore believed by most. This is why some of the opinions that were held as strong beliefs in the last century have been changed today.

Predictions: These are beliefs about the things that have not happened yet, but which our mind has decided would happen. If a student never reads, you believe that such student would fail even before he wrote the examinations. Across all spheres of life, we often have beliefs that have been made based on our predictions; an educated guess or just a plain inexplicable sense of certainty.

Broadly, for the purposes of this book, I will classify all beliefs into Positive and Limiting Beliefs.

1. Positive Beliefs: These are simply the beliefs that will do you good and empower you to move forward. They are beliefs that promote your improvement in life, and betterment as a person. Beliefs are not necessarily bad or good, it all depends on how you use them, and what you use them to achieve. A man who believes in God may learn to strengthen himself and always do his best just because he knows a God is watching. Another human who doesn't think God exists can also become strong and give his best since he knows there is no higher power to back him up. Therefore, this existential belief in a God, or non-existential belief both serve the same positive purpose for different people.

Positive beliefs strengthen you and give you power to achieve everything you set your mind to, beliefs that fill your mind with positive thoughts and free your mind of fear and hesitations. These are the beliefs you must hold on to. Examples of statements and beliefs that show a positive attitude that can drive you to success include:

- My life is in my hands, I am responsible for it.

- The next day will always be better than today.

- There is a space for me in the world.

- I am free to be me, and I can be my best version.

- I don't need people's approval to be the best in life.

- My thoughts have a way of changing my reality.

- I am different from the next man, our challenges are different, our life is different.

- I must make the best use of every situation I find myself.

- My hard work will be rewarded eventually, no matter how delayed it might seem.

- My past is behind me and it has passed; I must learn to look forwards.

- Failure is a lesson and an opportunity to improve and get better.

- Not everything is about me, everyone is not out to get me.

- I must constantly learn new things and get better at old ones.

- It is very important for me to forgive the hurt people have caused me, and not hold grudges.

- Nothing lasts forever. No matter how long I have something, I might lose it someday, so I better enjoy it.

- Everything doesn't have to be my fault; sometimes, things are just out of my control.

- I deserve to be happy.

2. Limiting Beliefs: There are beliefs and principles that that many people believe which have been the only thing keeping them away from real success. Like Jack in the opening story, so many persons are holding on to theories and rules that stop them from moving forward. Yet, they find it hard to recognize the source of their stagnancy. And if someone points this out, and advises them to change their beliefs, they get really defensive and refuse to change.

When you have an external problem, it is easy to solve it. But when your problem has to do with your mindset, such a problem can stay with you throughout your lifetime. That is why I often advise people that when they want to change their life, they must first change their core beliefs.

You might have heard of Vincent van Gogh. If you haven't heard of him, you probably will hear of him before you leave the world. He was a painter whose works sell for huge amounts of money these days. In fact, just four of his paintings have been said to have sold for more than one hundred million dollars. But do you know that when Vincent was alive, he believed himself to be so much of a failure that he even killed himself, just after he burned and destroyed many of his paintings? It was just soon after his death that his work finally gained recognition and financial success. This tragic story of Vincent has even been written as lyrics of popular songs. The only thing that held Vincent back, and denied the great man of witnessing his success was his limited belief in his own ability. He had limiting beliefs that made him hinge his life and happiness on the opinions and validation of other people. And when he didn't get it quickly enough, he lost all hope.

That, exactly, is what limiting beliefs do. They limit you and adversely affect your success and efforts.

How do we acquire our Beliefs?

We are born with zero beliefs but our beliefs are shaped by:

Parents: humans are born with minds that are free of thoughts and beliefs, and as we grow up in the care of our parents, we start picking up their beliefs and manner of life subconsciously until we are old enough to think for ourselves. And even then, most parents still teach their children their beliefs and demand that the children hold on to such beliefs. Common examples of such beliefs that are often handed down by parents include the existence of God, the law of sowing and reaping and the importance of earning money.

Relatives and Neighbours in the community also contribute to our beliefs through the general opinions that have been accepted by the individuals in our community.

Societal values and rules are often passed down to us by neighbours and relative. For example, an elderly man who lived beside our house when I was about twelve once told me that love would be easier if I have money, and he advised me to be rich; and I held on to the belief for many decades after that time.

Friends are one of the biggest influencers of the way we think and what we believe. Thus, it is quite easy for beliefs to be transferred between friends because of the trust that has already been established. The belief that everything will always work out eventually was told to me by a friend.

Teachers are the employed to change human thoughts and get their students to learn new beliefs. And good teachers do more than teach concepts and academics, they also transfer their core beliefs onto their students. Many people believe they must be academically good to be rich today just because their teachers repeated the same thing to them again and again. Even before most people get to travel through air and look down on the planet earth, teachers had taught the same belief as fact in their classroom.

Culture also plays a role in what we think and how we think. If your culture considers some things as abominations, you would most likely believe that you must never do those things. Some people have the beliefs that they must never eat while standing because their culture teaches them otherwise, some people believe that men are superior beings while I have heard of people who also believe that the womenfolk is superior. The two schools of thoughts were beliefs that were formed by two different cultures.

Books, Television, Newspaper, and the Internet are the major avenues that connect us to the world outside our bedroom, and especially in this age, ideas have become increasingly shared quickly from one end of the world to another. A good writer or speaker can share his opinions in another continent and be listened to or read some thousands of kilometers away. And if the ideas presented appeal to a listener or reader, a follower and firm believer may be gained.

Individual Experiences: We can also observe trends and changes on our own, and pick up some beliefs for ourselves. Studies suggest that as early as three months old, babies begin to understand how gravity works. They believe that if you throw a ball upwards, it will come back to the ground.

It is very important for me to state clearly that no matter the source of your beliefs, or the method you used to acquire them, it is **Test your beliefs**. A belief that cannot withstand being questioned and tested cannot be trusted to be true.

List of Limiting Beliefs

Limiting beliefs about **self** include:

- What people say about me is always the real truth about myself.
- I am not good enough.
- I cannot do it.
- People don't care about me.
- I am too ugly.
- Nothing about me attracts.
- People must show me respect.
- I do not deserve it.
- I don't want people to think of me like that.
- Nothing ever really changes.
- There is nothing anyone can say or do to change my mind.
- Nothing works for me.

Limiting beliefs about the world include:

- Nothing goes well in the world anymore.
- This world is filled with evil people.
- Nothing is fair.
- The world doesn't care if I die.
- War is the only thing the world understands.
- People from a particular country are never good.
- Religion is a problem in the world

- The colour of the skin determines a man's nature.
- I have no power to change the world.
- The world is too big for anyone to notice me.

Limiting beliefs about money include:

- It is evil to have a lot of money.
- Money destroys friendships.
- Riches attract troubles.
- No one can be rich without cheating others.
- Money is more important than love.
- Those who have money never have peace of mind.
- We use people to get money.
- Money is not important.
- Money is there for us to spend.
- My family has always been poor, so will I.
- Money can't buy happiness.

Limiting beliefs about the success include:

- I cannot handle success.
- I am going to fail, why other trying?
- No one has ever done it.
- I don't have enough brain to achieve it.
- Others have failed, I will too.

- It is too late.
- It is too difficult for me.
- If I get my hopes up, I will just be disappointed.
- Success lasts forever.
- I can't succeed without cheating.
- I always fail at first attempt.
- I just can't do it.

Limiting beliefs about the health include:

- I can't live long.
- My body is too old for this.
- This sickness will kill me.
- I need sickness to rest and recover.
- My health is not as important as work.
- Drugs make sickness worse.
- Only the young can stay healthy.
- Exercises are just a waste of time.
- Thinking too deeply can result in madness.
- Food is overrated.

Limiting beliefs about relationships include:

- A good relationship does not hard work, things go naturally.

- There is only one true love out there, you miss it once, you miss it for life.

- Everyone eventually leaves.

- When I go into a relationship, I might lose myself.

- I have to hold on to them, so they don't leave.

- No one will ever love me again.

- There is no good person out there for me.

- I will change him or her.

- He or she is too good for me.

- If he or she is the right person, I don't need to change anything about me.

- I need to be in a relationship to be happy.

How to Recognize Limiting Beliefs

Before you try to determine your limiting beliefs, it is important to identify the goals you have set, and understand why some beliefs of yours have been limiting you from achieving. And also, you must recognize which particular areas of your life your beliefs have been holding you back from excelling. Is it in your relationships, career or self? Once you can pinpoint the problem, it becomes less difficult to know the beliefs that have been limiting you.

You have to be deliberate in your action, and I will personally advise you to put pen to paper and make some notes. Ask yourself the following questions and give sincere answers.

What has always been the challenge, or blockade that stands on your way to achieving this goal? Is there a belief attached to this hindrance? Are there some of your thoughts that encourage the presence of these challenges?

When you think about your goal, what is the foremost thought that comes to your mind? Do you see reasons why you should not move forward, or do you see reasons why you must achieve the goals? Which emotions do you feel? Disappointment and fear, or excitement and motivation?

What will change about you and your relationships if you successfully achieve your goal?

And if you fail to achieve this goal, what do you think would have been the major reason?

I believe that within the answers you have provided to these questions, and from the things you have learnt before; there will be one or more limiting beliefs in your life.

And I would like to presume that you have identified some common beliefs from the ones I have listed.

How to Eliminate Limiting Beliefs?

After successfully identifying the limiting beliefs you have, you must determine to eliminate such beliefs from your life. Because the belief you have had for a couple of years have turned to habits, and a way of life, it may not be enough to just recognize such beliefs, and expect to stop living based on such beliefs.

It is not as simple and straightforward as that.

In order to successfully eliminate beliefs, you must first know why you hold such beliefs, you must identify the origin. Was this belief passed on to you by friends, parents or the community? Or did you pick it up as you went through life?

Once you have ascertained the origin of your limiting beliefs, you can then test such beliefs, and understand the reasons why they have been holding you back from achieving your dreams and goals. Any limiting belief that is put in doubt and questioned immediately starts to lose its power over your life.

The more you doubt such beliefs, the more they continue to crumble. And as you continuously gather facts and debunk the falsehood of such beliefs, you will soon let go of the limiting beliefs completely.

You may not become aware of the changes in your beliefs as soon as they happen, but close observation of your behavioural patterns and the thoughts of your mind will show you just how far you have come in getting rid of such limitations.

And then, you can really be free to live positively as you replace those limiting beliefs with new beliefs that will empower and strengthen you.

How to form New Empowering Beliefs?

I have been able to describe three steps involved in the formation of positive beliefs.

1. Identify and Accept the Beliefs: you may hear them being spoken or taught by another person, or maybe they creep into your mind, once you have thoughts that give you strength, you must identify such beliefs, and accept them. Accepting empowering beliefs involve allowing such believe to live in your mind by constantly thinking about such beliefs, and affirming them in your mind.

2. Believe the beliefs: Repeat such beliefs to yourself as much time as you can, write and post it everywhere, accept such beliefs as the truth, and see your past and your future in the light of such new beliefs. Once you believe a particular thought or belief, it automatically starts it work on you.

3. Practice: demonstrate the new belief you have adopted and let it show in your decisions and choices. Live by them until it becomes a part of you and begin to yield results. Go ahead and teach other people about this empowering belief, convincing them about your new manner of thinking and living.

I must advise you to be careful not to allow the beliefs you have successfully displaced from your mind and replaced with empowering thoughts return. This is why you need to continually disengage yourself from the limiting belief as you take up positive beliefs.

List of empowering beliefs about Money:

- I need money to help a lot people.
- Riches make happiness easier.
- I must earn as much as I can, and as early as possible.
- There is enough money in the world for everyone.
- I can be a billionaire too.
- Money solves a lot of problems.
- Making money is not as hard as people think.
- Money is freedom.
- I have everything I need to prosper.
- I need money to execute my ideas.

List of empowering beliefs about Self:

- There is nothing to be afraid of about tomorrow.
- I shape my own life.
- My past is who I was; I decide who I am now.
- The blessings in my life are more than the troubles
- Change is not always a bad thing.
- I must learn to forgive.
- I can always ask for help

- I can always get better.
- I deserve to be happy.
- It is possible for me to be perfect.

List of empowering beliefs about Success

- I will always find a way to overcome.
- In every challenge in life, there is something to learn.
- Mistakes are rehearsals for success.
- I have not achieved all I can yet.
- No dreams are too big for me.
- If I keep working hard, I will succeed.
- Talent is not enough to be successful.
- There is no success that doesn't require patience.
- Success never comes just by coincidence.
- I will always take my chances.

List of empowering beliefs about Relationship.

- I deserve to be loved.
- Love is a beautiful thing.
- Relationships can last.
- I value myself, and value others too.
- It is okay if it does not work out.
- There is no love without sacrifice.

- It is important to apologize quickly; it is a sign of strength.

- If I love someone, I should tell them.

- I must appreciate other people for their efforts.

- If someone says they are telling the truth, it is better not to doubt their words.

Get rid of Cognitive Biases: These are systemic errors in our thought process that translates into our decisions and judgements being wrong. One example of such cognitive biases is the Bandwagon effect, which causes a person to accept a certain belief just because a high number of people hold such belief. Stereotyping is another classic example of Cognitive bias. You must make a conscious effort to stop your mind from accepting a cognitive bias, and never allow your decisions be made on it.

Get rid of such bias.

Seven Life-Changing Beliefs

Everything happens for good: it is very important to hold this belief in your mind and live your life with confidence in it because it gives you a positive mindset to things, and helps you consider your options with a sound peaceful mind before making decision. It is especially important when things don't go your way, and you need to try again as it keeps your mind from losing its courage.

The World if full of abundance and gratitude is the

gate way to abundance: you must first believe that there are riches in the world before making plans to acquire those riches. And if you don't think there is an abundance of goodness in this world, the belief may stop you from getting any good. Gratitude is important to us because it allows us see and focus on our blessings as we make plans, rather than complaining about our needs.

I am responsible for everything that happens in my life; I am the Sculptor of my life, and the Master of my fate: this sound belief helps us to accept responsibilities over our lives. Once you realize and believe this, you will start to make smarter decisions, value your life more, and stop hoping for the universe to come to your aid- it almost never do.

Anything that my mind can conceive, my hand can achieve: I first considered this statement in my early twenties when I was trying to make concrete plans for my life. If you also believe this statement, like I do, you will see that your life has no limits, and you will constantly impress even your own self.

I am more powerful than your circumstances and problems: life, as is often the case, is littered with challenges here and there, and problems often raise their heads when we least expect them to. Yes; sometimes, you think you have everything covered only for an external factor to stand in your way. It is at those times that this belief will sound loud in your mind and encourage you to continue keeping on and forge ahead.

Three Things you must believe about your Goals, or you even don't bother having them at all.

1. It is possible to achieve them; believe in the possibility and have confidence that they are practicable and achievable by any human.

2. I am able to achieve them; believe in your personal ability to scale the heights, brave the storms, take on the challenge and hit your target.

3. I deserve to achieve them: believe that if anyone can achieve the goals, it has to be you. Tell yourself that you have everything needed to achieve the goal.

That is it: Possibility, Ability and Worthiness are three keys belief for achieving your goals.

As you set about changing your beliefs and starting a new chapter of positivity in your life, remember that every person, every experience (god or bad), every situation, every failure, every success and every opportunity comes in your life as a message from the universe to help you grow and realize your purpose.

Like the question W. Somerset Maugham asked, 'If you don't change your beliefs, your life will be like this forever. Is that good news?'

As the great man, Mahatma Gandhi said,

'Man often becomes what he believes himself to be.

If I keep on saying to myself that I cannot do a certain thing,

It is possible that I may end by really become incapable of doing it.

On the contrary, if I have the belief that I can do it,

I shall surely acquire the capacity to do it even if I may not have it at the beginning.'

CHAPTER
Three

Proscrastination

(The Common Enemy)

Charles Dickens, one of the greatest writers that ever walked the earth knew this enemy well enough to speak about it. 'Procrastination is the thief of time' he aptly said.

Consider that for a moment. This man was a legendary writer, he wrote so many novels, and published so many stories such that his fictional characters are even more popular than many Presidents of countries today, over two hundred years later.

Yet, this same accomplished writer knew all too well about procrastination and its devices. He was no stranger to this common enemy of humans.

The best ideas every conjured in the heart of men never came to light, and were never carried out, for this one reason- procrastination.

Some folks never said their last goodbyes to their loved ones just because of this one reason- procrastination.

Men and women who could have taken the first step in changing the world never did anything of repute just because they kept procrastinating.

What is Procrastination?

Let us look at what the Cambridge dictionary would say. It defines procrastination as 'the act of delaying something that must be done…'It is the putting off of an action that should be taken now until another time in the future.

Let us get something straight; procrastination is never good. And it is different, very different from planning.

I had an idea to write a book in 1997. The idea came to me like most great ideas come to men. I was travelling through the train and my left hand was clasped around a metal. As I felt the coldness of the metal against my head, I turned my attention to the feeling. But within a minute, I realized that the cold sensation had left my hand altogether.

It was a surprise to me, as I had never considered how easy it was for humans to adjust to their environment. And I realized that we are generally wired to respond to external changes and react to them. I was still lost in my thoughts when I realized that the seemingly insignificant observation I just made was a rule of life.

'Change your environment, change your life' the title of a book came to me as clear as day, and I was excited at the thought of writing such a book. Before the train got to my destination, I had written out a rough outline of the proposed book. The plan for the manuscript was very clear in my mind.

I thought I would start the book the following morning and I started to make plans for the new challenge.

However, at the end of that week, I had to get out of town for a program, so I told myself I would start the proper planning for the book when I returned.

When I returned two weeks later, I met the five pages of draft I had started to write on my table, and I smiled and promised myself to resume work on the book before the end of that week.

And that was what I did every weekend. I would walk around my study, pick up the five pages of draft, smile at the outlines I had written, and I would find a way to convince myself it was better to write the book at another time.

After three weeks, I stopped looking at the pages altogether, and I removed the pages from my work table, and placed it on the top of the shelf. Once within the next month, I took the pages off the shelf and realized I was not doing the right thing. So I decided to start the work afresh in the new year.

In January 1998, I moved out of my previous house and started to live in a new city. And for the next few months, I left many of my boxes unopened. As the time passed, I forgot about the book I had promised to write. When I finally opened the boxes, I returned the pages to the top of the shelf and convinced myself I had enough time to write it before the year ended.

It turned out I didn't.

I was walking past the library one afternoon when I noticed the books arranged on a table just outside the library. I walked closer to the table and looked at the cover pages of the books on display.

And then, I saw it. 'If you want to Change your Life, Change your Environment'. The words were written in bold black letter across the front of one of the books. I was astonished. I asked the woman behind the table if I could quickly look through the contents of the book, and she nodded and smiled.

When I checked the first pages and read through the table of contents, I realized that the book had been written based on the exact thoughts I had on the train.

I already started to think the author had stolen my ideas until I realized no one, not even my assistant, had seen the book or even heard about it.

And the realization brought along with it some regret. The ideas I had and didn't write had been placed on another mind by the universe. Just because of my procrastination, another person had written what I had planned to write.

When I returned home, I searched the top of my shelf, and I saw the five pages I had written still lying on my shelf. Procrastination had claimed yet another victim.

That one experience with procrastination was enough for my lifetime. I returned home shaken and in regrets. And I can assure you, it is that same result for all cases of procrastination- regret.

Other effects of Procrastination are:

- You may lose some opportunities that will never return till the end of your life:

We all know how valuable time is, and what happens when we waste it by putting off tasks till another date. There are so many opportunities that are time-based and would pass on if we don't do what we must quickly. When the stars align and everything seems right for you to take an opportunity, but you postpone and procrastinate, the simple fact is, the conditions may not be just right for the next couple of years, or ever. Since humans all have a limited time to spend in this world, it is important to seize the moment and do what we can in this time that has been given to us.

- You will fail to achieve your goals

  Goals are targets we set for ourselves and draw out plans of actions needed at particular times to achieve them. Thus, anytime you procrastinate one of these actions, the entire goal will be at risk of failure. Many people who failed just one of these actions because of procrastination often end up failing to achieve the goal altogether.

- Your career and relationship can be destroyed

  Procrastination is one of the leading causes of disappointment. And when disappointments become repeated, you lose trust and lose your integrity with it. What is a career or relationship without trust? It is nothing. No matter how the other party forgives you the first time you procrastinated and disappointed them, they most likely will not forgive in subsequent times. Statements like 'I will send the files tomorrow' and 'I will send the flowers another time' are examples of procrastinations that have affected lives negatively.

- It will make you lose your self-esteem

  Another thing procrastination does is that you end up being disappointed in yourself, as I was when I saw my idea published by another writer. When you cannot trust yourself anymore due to repeated procrastinations and disappointments, your self-esteem starts going down, and you will no longer be able to speak highly of your own ability in the presence of others.

- You will start making bad decisions

  Since you have procrastinated some tasks for a long time, when the deadline finally arrives and you are forced to make a move, your decision-making becomes hurried and not well thought out. This is why most bad decisions were made when people had been put under a lot of pressure to deliver within a short time.

- Your reputation will be ruined

  Once people get to know that you are the kind of person that often delays delivery in service, and never fails to do what you promised, they begin to doubt your every word, and it may be difficult to reassure them. And it won't be long before everyone begins to see you as a person who always fails to deliver.

- It increases stress and anxiety and may harm your health:

  Like I have said before, procrastination puts you under intense pressure when you have no other choice but to take a step. This often results in stress and anxiety that may hamper your health in the long run.

- It can cause guilt and depression

  If the feelings of disappointment, lack of trust in one's self, break in relationships and bad decisions become repeated and accumulate, it can ultimately lead to a feeling of guilt which can quickly give room for depression. Since procrastination is as a result of your inaction, any failure that comes as a result of it becomes your fault.

Why do you Procrastinate?

A recent study found that twenty one percent of people sincerely regard themselves as chronic procrastinators. So, why do so many people identify themselves as procrastinators? What happens in our mind that makes us put things off till another time?

Generally, we rely on our self-control mechanism I order to bring ourself to complete a task. This self-control centre of the brain receives its support from our motivation. However, when we experience demotivating factors or hindering factors, we may become exhausted mentally, and this may cause us to lose motivation and self-control. Once this happens, we tell ourselves that we can always do that task when our motivation returns.

But on the later time we have set, we consider again our motivation factors and compare it with the hinderance and the demotivating factors. If the demotivating factors outweigh the motivation, we lose our control and postpone the action.

And the cycle continues.

This is the reason why you don't pay your bills until sanctions are threatening, you don't start a task until the deadline is too near, or buy gifts until Christmas even.

Some other specific reasons why people procrastinate include:

- Goals that are not defined and written down
- Rewards that are too far in the future
- The feeling of being overwhelmed with too many tasks
- Anxiety about the result
- Perfectionism: waiting for the best time and the perfect conditions
- Obvious lack of self-discipline
- Lack of energy

- Fear of failure

- Sadness or lack of purpose

- Outright laziness

How to Overcoming Procrastination

1. Demystify your goals: break down the goal into small pieces of actions that are easily manageable and quickly achievable. For example, if you goal is to write a ten thousand words book, you can break the entire book into five hundred words per day, spread over twenty days, and you will achieve your target within three weeks. Rather than taking up a task at once and striving to complete it at a go, it is always helpful to divide such tasks into smaller portions

2. Make schedules for each task: It is always necessary to have a time for each task. This time must not be too far into the future or else, you may be tempted to continue to procrastinate. You can use tools like the calendar and reminders to make the process more efficient. If you have a plan to work on a monthly report, you can decide to write the report five days to the end of the month. And once that day comes, you are already prepared mentally to carry out your task.

3. Set personal deadlines: For the attainment of your goal, you must have a deadline. If you have to pay

bills on the last day of the year, it is better for you to set your personal deadline at a week to the end of the year. The personal deadline is useful since it safeguard you from disappointing people. Once the deadline you set for yourself approaches, you get more motivated to complete your task even when the actual date of delivery is not as near.

4. Get yourself started: One of the ways I have personally used to deal with procrastination is to start something, anything at all. You have to make sure you disobey the voice in your head constantly telling you to do everything tomorrow; no, start today and continue tomorrow. Once you are able to initiate the process and take the first steps, you overcome inertia and you get a firmer grasp of your self-control. For most people I have studied, it is easier to complete a task already started without procrastination.

5. Reward yourself: when you do a small bit of work that helps you get closer to your goal, reward yourself. If you want to start and finish a book quickly without procrastination, you can decide to reward yourself with a candy every time you finish a chapter. This boosts your motivation and gives you more strength to continue your task.

6. Focus on the goal, not the task: the goal is typically more appealing than the task; therefore, it is wise to pay attention to the goal while you carry out

your tasks. This helps you to complete your task as quickly as you can as you drive towards your goal. If you want to get a gift for a loved one and it seems you keep procrastinating, it will help you get motivated and act fast if you can imagine the smile on their faces when they receive the gift.

7. Become responsible to someone: one of the best ways to get rid of procrastination is to make sure you report to someone who you do not want to disappoint. It is better if this person is unrelated to the task, and can also rebuke you without fear. Sometimes, it is harder for us to disappoint others than to disappoint ourselves. This sponsor will closely monitor your schedules and keep track of your tasks so you don't procrastinate. And if you do, you might decide to apportion some form of fine or punishment for defaulting.

8. Step away from easy distractions: procrastination becomes quite easy when you have something more rewarding calling for your attention. And since the human mind finds some things more enjoyable that others, it can easily get carried away and distracted from a task. This is why you easily find yourself opting to play games even when you have some important schedules to meet up with.

9. Gather your resources: one of the ways you can use to defeat procrastination is by making your work easier so that your motivation and ease of task

becomes great enough to overcome your mental laziness. One of the ways to make work easy is by getting your resources needed for the work available and easily accessible. Once your mind finds it easy to do a task, your body also responds and stops the procrastination.

10. Switch tasks at interval: the human mind quickly gets bored of a particular line of action when such action is carried out repeatedly and continuously. You can overcome this tendency to procrastinate by switching your mind from one task to another intermittently so that you can overcome the monotonous feeling that brings boredom and makes you procrastinate.

As you make the decision today, to get a hold of your life and be in control of your destiny. Don't put aside the troubles of today till tomorrow; the troubles only get more difficult, and tomorrow already has troubles sufficient for it.

Never forget the words written by Benjamin Franklin, 'You may delay, but Time will not.'

CHAPTER
Four

Self-Sabotage

There is this story of a woman who had been sacked from her last two jobs. The reason for dismissal was always the same; she did not take the job seriously enough. I always found it had to believe anytime she told me about the termination of contracts. In fact, the second time she lost her job, I had to tell her to show me the sack letter before I could believe she was indeed sacked.

I have always known this woman since she and I attend same lectures in the first year of college. She was always the first person into the class, always took notes, and never missed a class all through the years we spent in the institution. So it was quite hard for me to imagine that such a hardworking and committed person would not take her job seriously.

After the second dismissal, I met her and tried to ask her the reasons why the companies who had fired her in the past had done so. In replying, she told me maybe she wasn't the right fit for the job.

I went ahead and asked her to tell me the kind of job she wanted, and she gave me a list of choices of jobs which she felt she would do very well at. I took note of the list and spoke with a friend who ran a company at the centre of the city.

I stood for her and assured my friend that she was a committed worker. When he asked why she was retrenched from her last jobs, I also him those employers were not patient enough to see her best efforts. We were finally able to find her a position in the company and she started working again. She thanked me profusely, told me it was her dream job, and promised me to give her best.

But just three weeks later, my friend called me around 10pm on a Tuesday and told me she had just got to work at that exact time- a company whose resumption time was 8 am. She went two hours late!

My friend went further to inform me that she only arrived to work early in the first week of employment; and that she had been coming late since the start of the second week.

My friend also told me that if she didn't change by the end of that week, he was going to sack her.

I apologized on her behalf and called her some hours later. I tried my best to explain to her not to disappoint me. And I also admonished her to get more serious with work and arrive as early as possible.

She answered me mechanically and said she would try. But the very next day, she was sacked. It turned out she only arrived at work at past ten in the morning.

When I spoke with her, she told me pointblank that she didn't know why she kept going to the office late. And when I pressed her further, she just smiled and said she would get another job.

It was the very first time I saw clearly how humans sabotage their own selves and destroy good opportunities with their own hands. This was a woman who always arrived early for classes and services, but the job she claimed was her dream job, she threw it away and said she didn't know why she went late to work. By her own doing, she made sure she lost her job.

What is self-sabotage? And how do you know if you are it affects you?

Humans are a complex being; and our minds are even more complicated. Self-sabotaging behaviours include actions, decisions and thoughts that we generate by ourselves which work against our goals and creates problems for our lives. They are deliberate or subconscious things we do that have opposite effects on our plans and hopes.

When you find yourself always asking the questions, 'Why am I doing this to myself?', 'What is wrong with me?' and 'Why do I keep getting in my own way?', it is very likely that you are a victim of self-sabotage.

You plan to take a relationship to the next level tomorrow, but today, you refuse to pick his or her phone calls for no just reason, and you pick a fight over his or her habit of picking the nose.

You plan to take the next step in your career by turning in a paper or presentation, but you find yourself postponing writing the paper or preparing the presentation.

You have been told you would be given an opportunity to show your ability only if you can maintain a certain weight limit, but you inexplicably kept eating high-calorie meals with high fat content that increase your weight.

A child has been doing well and his future has been promising. He has good grades and receives the love and support of his parents, but just before he leaves high school, he begins to experiment with drugs and changes his lifestyle. He deliberately stayed out of school, flunked his exams and changed his friends for no just cause.

You want to change your lifestyle and go on diets for six months, but after the first month, you take an extra bottle of drink, an extra size of pizza or a eat a bar of chocolate. And then, just because of this, you decide to cancel the entire program and just overeat.

These are all classic cases of self-sabotaging decisions and actions. Conflict, procrastination, laziness and any habit that hamper your health are all different methods people use to self-sabotage themselves.

Generally, you know you self-sabotage when you achieve a long-term goal of yours, and find a way to mess everything up and destroy the opportunity somehow.

It can also be observed in people who keep quiet and refuse to step up and show their best version when called up and given a chance to do so.

Self-sabotage leads to failure, misery, dissatisfaction with life, poverty, guilt, sadness and in extreme cases, suicide.

Ten indicators of self-sabotage include the following:

- Procrastination
- Inaction
- Not asking questions
- Conflicts or fights
- Lateness
- Self-injury
- Bad temper
- Hesitation and indecisiveness
- Self-pity and Isolation
- Oversleeping

Why do people self-sabotage?

The one answer to this question will be for me to say 'The feeling of being unworthy' but I will like to also explain some other reasons.

1. Feeling Unworthy: people sometimes receive gifts they do not deserve, and when that happens, what humans do is to try and throw the substance away while looking for something that they feel they have earned. It is the same thing for people who self-sabotage. When they acquire something good and attain a goal, they suddenly begin to feel that they are not worthy of such success, and often find one way or the other to get that good thing destroyed.

2. Foolish hunger for excitement: when boredom sets in, no matter how good or beautiful something is, the human mind starts getting tired and begins to seek for excitement. This is what happens to people who have the best partners in life, but still cheat on their partners just because they have grown so accustomed to the partner and they want to feel the excitement of living life on the edge. When people achieve a dream, they may begin to feel uninspired and bored of living their dream, and begin to push their luck until they destroy their dream.

3. Need to be in Control (even of your own failure): people may begin to feel that they are lacking real control of things when everything is going well with them. And the need to be in full control of their lives may push them to sabotage their present success just so they can prove to themselves that they engineered their own failure. This is the reason why you may choose to scream at your boss, bang your hands on his office desk and curse him as you resign from a job that has working well for you.

4. Looking for Change: just for the sake of it, there are people who also end a good thing in their live. Just because they want to see something new, they destroy the old source of their happiness and take up a new one. I have seen people who started to experiment with something harmful to their body

just because they wanted to change something about their lives.

5. Guilt: if your mind keeps telling you that you are responsible for a something bad, and you keep blaming yourself, it won't be long before you start looking for a way to punish yourself out of guilt. And very often, people mete out punishments to themselves by destroying everything good about them until they feel they have received the consequences they deserve. Some can even go as far as inflicting bodily harm on themselves.

6. Hopelessness: when you start a task and lose all hope of it succeeding halfway through, the next thing some people do is to destroy their achievement altogether in the hope that they start again. When some things are not working to your favour and you begin to consider putting an end to everything, you are self-sabotaging yourself. This is often seen I couples who go out of their ways to make each other mad and hurt each other just because they feel things are no longer working out and have lost hope in their relationship,

7. Fear of Success: as I have said in previous chapters, some persons fear success and become afraid and anxious when they think about making progress. These people can sometimes destroy promising projects in their lives as they act on their fear while trying to protect themselves from anything their

mind has conjured up as a reason to be afraid of success. Though I have found out that this happens subconsciously, when you fear success, you find a way to make sure you never attain it.

8. Shame: one of the examples of self-sabotaging actions is the refusal to step up and show your ability when called upon. And this is often because you are ashamed of yourself or of your ability. When you feel inadequate or insecure, you may self-sabotage the good opportunities in your life through your inaction.

9. External Criticism: while criticism can sometimes be constructive and help, most criticisms can make a person so hurt and sad that he completely shuts off and destroy the good things that have been unfairly criticized. A football player or musician who has been sorely criticized for a performance may decide to deliberately underperform or quit just to get back at the critics. This is also self-sabotage.

10. Mental Illness is one other reason that explains why people ruin some of the best things in their lives.

Overcoming Self-sabotage

Since it has become obvious that this act of destroying all the good things in your life will only deny you of success, kill your self-esteem, reduce your productivity and lead you to failure in life, it is necessary for me to teach you how you can get over the destructive tendencies. The most important first step to solving this problem is to examine yourself, recognize that you are a victim of your own negative actions, and accept that it is something you have to deal with. Think on the different reasons I have stated above and identify which ones are very common to you. And then, determine in your mind to conquer this obvious weakness.

Some steps you can take to gain freedom from self-sabotage include:

- Redefine Success: you have to reassess yourself and examine what success means to you. Measure success in the long-term, remember that your goal is only complete when you retire and finish up everything; don't sabotage your success before then.

- Rule over your mind: self-sabotaging decisions take up their roots in the mind. If you can get a hold of your thoughts, and take control of your mind, you can always have the power to stop yourself from destroying your blessings.

- Express your feelings: stop keeping things bottled up in your mind, show your true self and share your thoughts. If others are aware of your goals, they may stop you from killing it.

- Conquer your fears: when you feel insecure and become afraid of succeeding, it is that time you must convince yourself that you are able to overcome such fears while assuring yourself of managing your success well.

- Let go of past and Live in the present: everyone is ashamed of something in their past. We all have made decisions which were wrong, but when you refuse to accept this and let it go, you start believing you don't deserve something good, and self-sabotage sets in. You can conquer this by living in the present and enjoying the good things you have now.

- Stop comparison: I will talk more on this later. When you keep measuring yourself based on the achievements of other people, you will always see yourself as a failure and destroy the little successes you have already recorded.

- Treat yourself better: once you realize you deserve the good things of life, you begin to treat yourself better and do your best to preserve every positive achievement, rather than destroy them.

- Accept that you are imperfect: humans have their shortcomings and limitations, and you are no different. Once you accept your imperfections and realize there are times when you will disappoint yourself, you will learn to treat yourself better.

- Be considerate of others: if the woman in my opening story had considered me and thought about the fact that I stood for her before she got the job, maybe she wouldn't have been so quick to self-sabotage.

- Get professional help: therapists, counselors and psychologists may have to step in and be of help to you especially when your self-sabotaging is getting to the level of substance abuse, depression and suicidal thoughts.

CHAPTER
Five

Self-Doubt and Negative Self-Talk

'If you hear a voice within you saying,
"You cannot paint",
Then by all means paint
And that voice will be silenced.'

—Vincent Willem van Gogh.

And that, my friend, is the way you treat all cases of self-doubt.

Self-doubt is explained in the Oxford's Advanced Learner's Dictionary as the feeling that you are not good enough. Negative self-talk is a reflection of self-doubt and a consequence of it. Once you continue to belittle your abilities and doubt if you can achieve something, you will begin to speak the same belief into reality.

'As a man thinks in his heart, so is he.' It is a true verse from the Christian Holy Bible, and it hold true for all humans. Once you doubt yourself and feel defeated and unable, the next stage is to speak out your doubt and profess negative talks. And once this happens, you become actually defeated in life.

But it all starts from the mind as self-doubt.

A man who speaks negatively and doesn't believe in himself cannot be motivated enough to achieve anything. If you don't believe in yourself, no one will believe in you; and you will not do anything good in life.

I attended a Mathematics class with my best friend when I was preparing for my high school certificate exam. We had been classmates for four years, and we have always read together in preparation for the exam. Two weeks to the exam, we wrote a preparatory test and while I score 82 percent, he had 75 percent. I was happy and became confident about passing the Mathematics exam. But my friend was not.

He started to complain about his test score and told me he was not sure he would pass the exam. When he told me this, I was shocked to hear him. the pass mark of the Mathematics exam was 50 percent, and I had thought that his score of 75 percent in the test should make him more confident about his ability. But maybe because he scored less than me, he started to doubt if he was any good.

I was certain at that time that he was good enough to perform excellently in the Mathematics exam; I knew he was good at Mathematics. In fact, we had always scored similar scores in previous exams. He was good enough.

We went for the exam and wrote the Mathematics in the same examination hall. Before we got in, my friend still insisted that he was not sure he would do well. When I reminded him of his ability and the fact that he had never failed any exams in the past, he shrugged and didn't utter a word.

After the exams, he walked up to me and simply said, 'I told you I wouldn't do well.'

I told him to wait for the result before making the conclusion.

Some weeks later, the results of the High School Examinations were released. I checked my result and had 80 percent in Mathematics.

My friend checked his. He had 48 percent. I didn't know how the score came about or what happened. But what I know is, he believed he would fail, he doubted his ability, he confessed negatively, and that was exactly what happened. He failed.

This was a boy who had never score below 50 percent in his entire academic history.

I knew without any doubt that he failed because of his doubt and negative confession.

And I am assuring you today, once you start to doubt yourself and speak negatively, you will not achieve anything.

Some negative self-talk statements are

- I cannot do anything
- I am not worth it
- It is all pointless
- They will hate me
- I will fail
- I am completely to blame

- Maybe I am stupid

- I can't learn

- This is not for people like me

- I can't be better than my parents

How to overcome self-doubt

- Get better, Improve: If you keep doubting your ability, the next thing to do is to find ways to get better. Instead of allowing your self-doubt continue, attack it and improve yourself until you feel confident.

- Celebrate small achievements: doubts arise when you feel you can't achieve something. But if you learn to enjoy your little accomplishments, you will believe in yourself more, and become confident of overcoming bigger challenges.

- Stop the comparison: when you keep looking at others, you will start to magnify your shortcomings. So, stop comparing yourself with others; no two persons are the same.

- Don't take criticisms personal: when people make harsh assessment about your competence and ability, it is not that time you start to doubt yourself. No; instead, it is the time you must believe in yourself more and prove them wrong.

- Stop all excuses: excuses strengthen your doubts, and validate them. But if you can quit making such excuses and trust in your ability, it becomes easier to let go of self-doubt and start believing in yourself.

How to stop negative self-talk

1. When you speak negatively, be aware it is wrong for you to have said that, and immediately, say the opposite over and over again. In this way, you are teaching your mind stop generating those kinds of thought.

2. Make a list of positive statements, paste them in your room, and speak them into the air every morning, and every evening. This way, you will force your mind to shift from negativity to positivity.

3. Engineer your thoughts to produce only positive thoughts. No words escape a man's lips without passing through the mind. Heal the mind, heal the lips. Read books that encourage positive beliefs and focus on the positive aspects of your life.

CHAPTER
Six

Worry

*"I am an old man and have known a great many troubles,
but most of them never happened."*

—Mark Twain

Much like Mr. Twain, a lot of us have formed the worrying habit of worrying too much.

One of the most complete definitions of worry is, 'to feel anxious or troubled about actual or potential problems.'

I find this definition complete because it doesn't only cover actual problems; it also covered the potential problems that only exist in our minds. Look at the words of Mark Twain; he had many troubles but he was quick to note that most of these his problems never even happened.

And even the ones that happened, worrying about them didn't solve a thing.

So far life and its events remain uncertain, humans will always worry about their future- whether actual or potential.

Most worries come in form of questions. How will I make enough money? What if they find out about my past? What are they saying about me? I am getting old, what have I achieved? What if I don't make it? Will this method and plan work? Is my friend getting better? Am I safe? What if I make a mistake? Why am I so unlucky? What if everything goes wrong? Am I good enough? Will everything be alright? Will I meet my target, will I achieve my goal? Will I ever find love? Why am I still single? Will I do well?

These are questions we have asked ourselves at one time of our life or the other. But you know what? A study proves that 85 percent of what we worry about never happen.

What then do we accomplish when we worry? The question has a simple answer- Nothing.

Other than the fact that worrying hinders your success and motivation level and stops you from achieving what you want, it adds absolutely nothing to your future or the solution.

Why then do we worry?

Worrying is not one of the attributes we were born with; far from it. In fact, we begin to only worry after the age of four or five, depending on each child's development. And up till the age of eight, most children only worry about their academic grades and whether their friends and parents would leave or stay.

But once the teenage years start and a child begins to grow into an adult, more questions begin to pop up in the mind and we start to think about our future. From this stage till death, different worries come to the mind; from little things like wrinkles and haircut to big things like parenting and marriage.

But no matter the reason for the worry, the one thing that is common to all is the fear of uncertainty. Like I have explained before in the chapter of Fear, fear is a feeling brought to our mind in a bid to prepare the mind and protect it.

When your mind starts wondering about what might happen, and you begin to think deeply about a question, rolling it over and over in your mind, it will quickly become something to worry about.

According to statistics, the typical adult mostly worries about work or career, money or debt, health, time or being late, relationship, safety or security, being respected and social media presence.

How can you overcome worry?

- Accept that worry has never helped anyone, and it will never help you.
- Enjoy the present and take time to savour each moment.
- Instead of looking for things to worry about, find good things to be grateful for.
- Make a plan for the future, create a checklist and act out your plans.
- Accept that you cannot always be in charge, and that some things are out of your control.
- Have faith and believe that things will work out for you; have a positive outlook about life.

- Once you have given your best and done something, put your mind off it and concentrate on new tasks.

- Stop thinking about what others think of you. Stop getting too interest in other people's opinion about you.

- Stop overthinking situations and trying to understand everything that happens.

- Have patience. Be strong enough to wait for the future to become clearer to you.

- Be grateful for what you have and celebrate your achievements.

- Tell people about your worries and ask for their help.

The list I have made above is not too different from what the great American philosopher, Ralph Waldo Emerson, wrote in a letter he sent to his daughter when he saw her worrying over a mistake she'd made.

This is what the letter says:

"Finish each day and be done with it. You have done what you could. Some blunders, losses, and absurdities no doubt crept in; forget them as soon as you can.

Tomorrow is a new day; let today go so you can begin tomorrow well and serenely, with too high a spirit to be encumbered with your old nonsense. Each new day is too dear, with its hopes and invitations, to waste a moment on yesterdays."

If you know you worry too much, maybe you ought to consider pasting those words in a corner of your room.

Neither yesterday nor tomorrow deserves your worry.

Live in the present and work with a good plan.

And you will be alright eventually.

CHAPTER
Seven

Comparison

"Comparison with myself brings improvement, comparison with others brings discontent."

—Betty Jamie Chung

When I was about eight, my sister and I attended the same school, and each morning, my mother sends us off after placing ten cents in my hand and five cents in hers. She explained that it was because I was older, that I should get a bit more than my six-year-old sister.

My younger sister never complained; I never saw her pout or cry just because the money given to me was more than hers.

But some months later, as we got ready for school, my mom called me and gave me the usual ten cents. And I ran off to school. But before I could go far, she called me back and told me to wait for my sister. I waited until she caught up with me and we walked to the school together.

Just halfway to the school, I asked my sister if she kept her money well, and she said yes.

I didn't know why but I asked her how much she was given. She hesitated for a moment before she answered and told me it was ten cents. Immediately, I became very angry.

'Mom said it was because today is my birthday, and I should spend the rest with my friends.' She explained.

I knew it was indeed her birthday, but it didn't stop my anger.

In that instant, I looked upon the ten cents in my hands with hatred. My anger rose so much that I began to scream at my sister, asking why she should get the same amount of money as me.

The joy I had felt up till that point evaporated quickly and I stared hard and long at the ten cents of my younger sister.

And then, in foolish fury, I threw away the ten cents that my mother had given to me out of her little, and I stormed off. My sister ran after me, and pleaded with me to wait for her. But I did not.

Just because she had the same money as me on her birthday, I became discontent and even angry at my own gifts, and threw it all away.

Though the story above happened many decades ago, and I now knew better, I still get ashamed of myself anytime I remember the event.

But it is an instructive story, isn't it? It is the story of all the people who compare themselves with others.

Comparison involves the consideration of the similarities and difference between one entity and another. When you look at your, look at another person's life and check the differences, you are comparing.

People often compare themselves with another person using attributes they can observe and use for measurement.

For example, personality, looks, status, position, power, body, intelligence, bank balance, career, dressing sense, lifestyle, achievements , income, talent, communication skills, academic performance, health and almost every other physical attribute.

The rate at which humans compare with other people has never been as high as this age of internet and social media; where you gather friends and followers and each person shows their good sides and tell their good stories. If you are not careful, you will easily fall into the temptation of measuring yourself with their standards without considering if those standards are real, or if these people are doing all that to hide the worst things about them.

I can assure you that, for most of the people you compare yourself with, if you can only see their full picture and hear their full story, you will realize that you have a better life.

Adverse effects of comparison

- You become discontent with what you've got. It is just like what happened to me in the story when I realized my sister had same amount of money as me. Hardly can you see anyone who doesn't feel not good enough once they shed light on other people and focus on the positives on their lives. No matter how good your own life actually is, no matter how happy and satisfied you have always been with your life, once you start to compare your achievements or looks with another person, you start seeing that you are lacking in many areas. This is why comparison never ends well. It only steals your Joy.

- Damages self-esteem: as a consequence of you successfully convincing yourself that you are lacking and not good enough, your self-esteem drops drastically and you start losing faith in yourself. You begin to hesitate when given a chance to show your worth, and you lose confidence in your ability as the picture of the person you have been comparing yourself with gets stuck in your mind.

- It never inspires: once you start to measure your success with the success of other people, you start building your decisions on them and begin to imitate their methods. You lose your inspiration and consider their life as a template to live yours. Your ideas become bad ideas when considered in the light of the other people. But the thing is, once you use a person as a standard, you can never measure up.

- It limits you and you never realize your true potential: it is as simple as that. Since you have chosen to abandon your peculiarities and your true self while trying to measure your life using other people's scales, both your abilities and potentials go to waste. You will not achieve what you have been built to achieve but instead, you will destroy your life while trying to be like others. And even if you can manage to be like them, you will never have same fulfillment.

• Breeds inferiority complex: if you compare yourself to the twenty persons in your group, and you find yourself falling short of their standards, you will automatically consieder than far better than you, and this is where inferiority complex begins. It doesn't matter if you can play the piano better than the twenty people, you will feel less of a human to them since your mind as been deceived to think you are not as good as them.

• Causes superiority complex: sometimes, very few times, your may believe you are better than others because of a single thing in your life you have chosen to compare them with. If you are taller than everyone else, you may start feeling you are better than them as a human. This leads to pride and self-aggrandizement until your ego puts you on your backside and you are humiliated because of your false sense of importance.

• Lack of self acceptance and self-love: since you constantly see things in your life that are too bad, you will never love yourself for being who you are.

Instead, you will loathe the attributes in you which you have assumed makes you fall short.

- And ultimately, comparison will give room to negative emotions like jealousy, envy, anger and insecurity. It is just like I did in my story. I was jealous of my sibling, I was angry at her for no just cause, and I wasted the gift that had been given to me.

How do you stop comparing yourself with others?

1. Focus on yourself. The whole concept of comparison is a shift of focus towards other people. Therefore, if you can successfully shift attention to yourself and seek to improve your abilities and get better just for your own sake, you will be free from comparison. You have to realize that life is not a competition with others. Since you a have different DNA from the next human, you must not expect the same life.

2. Explore and appreciate your uniqueness; realize that the difference you notice between you and another person is all a part of makes you special and sets you apart from the rest of the world. No one can be a better version of yourself. Learn to accept yourself for who you are while you do your best to get better in every way. And as you do this, rather than looking at the physical attributes of

another, pursue the greater things in life like love and service, which have no measurement scales.

3. Recognize your intelligence and focus on your success: some have abilities to draw or paint, some other have the talent to sing or teach, some are mentally gifted and make sound advisers, and others have outward attributes as their only asset. You have to identify which group you belong, and what you are great at. Don't try to define your intelligence or success by other people's standards. Like it is said, if you judge a fish by its ability to climb a tree, he will live all its life thinking he is stupid.

4. Accept that someone will always be better than you at something. It is the rule of life; we have different measures of gifts, we have divers skills. There will always be people who will do better and achieve more than you. But the secret is to look at what you have which they don't. There is usually something you can do better than the other people. Once you believe this, you will not feel the need to measure up to other people whenever you feel that they are better than you. It is normal, and it is not holistic.

5. Realize that no one has a perfect life. I repeat, no one, not a single person in this world, not the president of the country, not the famous musician on tour, not even the monk hidden away from civilization, no one, not a single person has a perfect life. It is

not possible for humans to be an all-round perfect life. And this is a fact of life. No matter how it may seem that someone else is living a perfect life, they are not. That is a fact.

CHAPTER
Eight

Instant Gratification

*'Don't give up what you want most for
what you want now.'*

—Anonymous

'I want it badly and I want it now!' that statement is the summary of instant gratification. It is feeling of strong desire to experience pleasure and get fulfilled without delay.

Psychologically, we all respond and act based on the pleasure principle which convinces us to pursue our needs and urges until we feel gratified. And when we don't get these urges satisfied, tension and anxiety replaces the hunger.

In the same vein, humans are also generally wired to find all the possible ways to avoid pain.

When you perceive the smell of a nice food, your stomach rumbles and you follow the sweet smell of the food. You get the food, and eat it until your desire is satisfied. Your body relaxes afterward.

You have been underwater for some moment and need to breathe in air. So you swim up as quickly as you can and you open your mouth wide and gulp in air. Your body relaxes afterward

You see a woman who has a nice body shape, and your eyes follow her around. Your mind start desiring to have her and be with her, your body also responds. You try all you can to convince her to sleep with you and you have sex. Your body relaxes afterward.

You feel the urge to have a smoke but there are no cigarettes in your pocket. You ask around and no one has. You run along to the next shop and buy a packet of cigarette. You light it up and take in the first long smoke and puff it out. Your body relaxes afterward.

You see that a new product of a phone is out. Your find out the price and realize you cannot afford it. You desire to have the phone and you borrow money from a friend to get it. You queue up until you buy the phone. Once you open the case and get the new phone in your hand, your body relaxes.

These are all examples of instant gratification. You want something, and you want it as soon as possible. Your mind and body feel restless and discontented until your want is met. As you have noticed, one common thing to all the examples is that the body relaxes after the desire has been gratified.

That is what is called the pleasure and reward pathway. It involves a network of nerves which are responsible for responding to the stimulus of want and desire by giving the feeling of reward and gratification that often comes as pleasure. The higher the dopamine, a neurotransmitter in the brain, released in the brain, the higher the extent at which a human is willing to go to satisfy a need.

We all want our desires and urges to be satisfied now and the temptation is often too strong for most people to overcome. This happens because our instinct hates delays and we are impulsive by nature. We were not born with self-control and we already start to anticipate the satisfaction of the urge even before we get it, imagining the desire being satisfied as we pursue it.

The Marshmallow experiment on instant gratification

Though this experiment has been faulted and debunked based on recent findings, I will like you to understand it and pick a thing or two.

In the early 1970s, a team of psychologists in Stanford designed a study where they offered children a choice to either take a marshmallow now and leave, or wait for another fifteen minutes and then take two marshmallows. After the experiment, the children were divided into two groups based on whether they choice to take one now, or wait and take two. In follow-up studies, it was discovered that some years later, the group who chose to delay gratification had better lives measured in form of education than those who chose instant gratification.

In my years in this world, I have learnt that people who have the ability to control their desires and put their body under control are more likely to succeed than those who run at every opportunity to satisfy their wants.

And I don't think I need an experiment to prove it.

Why must you stop instant gratification?

- It hinders you from achieving your goals: since goals are often made in the long-term and would always require a bit of time, instant gratification pushes us into abandoning our goals while we chase immediate satisfaction. For example, the woman who went into a diet control programme for weight loss, she will always be tempted by the nice pictures of high-calorie foods which are often sweet and give a lot of pleasure. And once you promise yourself to read a book per week, the instant need to check up on social media will distract you from achieving your goal.

- It weakens our mind, will power and self control: since we pursue instant gratification, and never refuse our desires, no matter how vain or destructive, our mind becomes weak and we lose all our will power. If this goes on for a long time, you would soon find that you have become addicted and lost all self-control.

- It makes you impatient and lazy as you lose your ability to wait and work. Most of the things that your body seeks immediately are things that will not require any work. This is why a man would rather satisfy his urge for sex with a prostitute or one-night stand than cultivate a relationship or get married. Instant gratification always takes the easy way out, and it never waits.

- It denies you of lasting happiness: smoking cannot bring you lasting happiness, but a good pair of lungs can. A new phone cannot make you happy for long, but a life free of debt can. As you strive to achieve instant rewards and get your desires immediately fulfilled, you are denying yourself of the happiness you could have felt more in the future.

The opposite of instant gratification is delayed gratification. Rather than thinking of the short-term, you think of the long-term. Rather than getting the little joy now, you get a lasting joy later. Rather than getting what you want, you get what you really need.

What are some methods and strategies to overcome habit of instant gratification and achieve delayed gratification?

1. Distract yourself until the desire passes, it will pass. I know the temptation is often very strong, and you may feel you would die if you don't satisfy those instant desires, but I want you to know that you will survive. And the desire, no matter how strong now, will pass. So, take a walk, get a book and read, go into the midst of people, go outside, visit friends, do your hobby, distract yourself and take off your mind from the desire until it passes. Once you do this once, it gets easier to achieve subsequently.

2. Remind yourself of the consequences: when you feel the strong desire to indulge in instant gratification,

it is often helpful to remember what you stand to lose if you satisfy those urges. The thought of losing so much and being negatively affected just because of a few minutes or days or pleasure may stop you.

3. Try to be logical: ask yourself if it makes sense to go into debt just for the sake of a new gadget, does it make sense to cut short your decision of over a month just because of a few minutes of pleasure? Instant gratification always go against commonsense and wisdom. Once you can be logical and really consider all the perspectives, you will see reasons to stop.

4. Get an alternative source of enjoyment. If you are on a diet, rather than a bar of chocolate or a bowl of ice cream, get a bowl of dates and chew on them. If you are trying to quit substance addiction, eat a bar of chocolate or a bowl of ice cream instead of taking drugs. The goal is to break the reward pathway, refuse to allow your body control your life, and overcome instant gratification.

CHAPTER
Nine

Lack of Passion and Purpose

'Passion is the genesis of genius.'

—Tony Robbins

'If you can't figure out your purpose, figure out your passion. For your passion will lead you right into your purpose.'

—T. D. Jakes.

The Merriam-Webster Dictionary aptly defined Passion as 'a strong feeling of enthusiasm or excitement for something or about doing something.' And it also defined Purpose as 'the reason why something is done or used, the aim or intention of something, or the feeling of being determined to do or achieve something.'

That is why I will completely agree with T. D. Jakes who tied these two important elements together and stated that passion will lead you to purpose. Why? Because if you find something which you have a strong feeling of enthusiasm to do, and you keep doing that something, you will easily make it your purpose in life, and consider that same something as the reason why you are alive.

A musician has the passion to sing, and she makes it her life's purpose to bring music and joy to millions of people.

A comedian knows he is very funny and has a passion to see people laugh, and he decides to dedicate his life to spreading laughter and happiness throughout the word.

A doctor realizes early in life that she loves to care for people and ease their pain, so she makes it her life's goal to care for, treat, and heal as much people as he can.

A man discovers he has the passion to lead people, he finds excitement in guiding people, so he decided to spend the rest of his life in politics, holding government positions from the age of 30 to the age of 70.

History mostly only remembers the people who dedicated their lives to achieve one goal, and pursing a purpose with all the passion and zeal they could muster.

When you find something you love and do it to get excitement and fulfillment for yourself, that is passion. But when you extend it to other people and to do it for the world, it becomes purpose.

It is very important to live with passion and purpose or else, you find yourself going through life as a spectator who drifts around endlessly without aim. You will lack motivation, and will not enjoy real success and happiness.

Until you find your passion and pursue it, you will not be able to record excellence and fly as high as you can. Even if you succeed at something you are not passionate about, that success will be limited and very brief. Your satisfaction and the joy you derive will not be deep and long-lasting.

Passion is the fuel, nay, it is the vehicle, that drives you through life especially when the wind and storm of obstacles threaten to overcome you.

Louise was always invited to sing for her church whenever they hold concerts; and it was an open secret that she was one of the best singers in the town. She would sing in some places, and tears would streak down the face of strong men. And she did all these while she was still in High School. She already had plans to turn her passion into purpose and make the world her audience.

But tragedy struck two months before she left school, and she lost her father. It was her father who got her her first guitar, and she was her sponsor and motivation. She barely had enough energy to write her final exams but she still managed to get the required grades.

Two years later, she was working as a receptionist at one of the hotels in the town. She earned enough to take care of her mother and two siblings, and she worked hard as she could. She woke up very early in the day, and slept when it was dark because she did night shifts in another restaurant.

Her two jobs wore her out but she felt comforted whenever she saw her siblings having a good life. Some nights, she would take out her guitar and play tunes that brought tears to her eyes and her mother's. The tears were from the thought of what could have been.

She had stopped to sing, but she still sang for her family sometimes. And they all knew it was her passion, and her life. But because she couldn't achieve it, nothing could replace the emptiness she felt on such nights.

She was in the lobby of the hotel on one morning when she hummed the tune of a popular song and a woman heard. The woman looked some few years older than her mother, and when the woman asked her if she could sing the song for her, she slowly nodded and said yes.

The woman quickly drew nearer and listened as Louise sang with a low voice. But it was enough.

The song was about love and sadness, and the woman sniffed and looked at her with moist eyes when she finished. She asked her why she wasn't singing for a living, and Louise told her the short version of her life story. The woman gave her a card and promised her she would be back at the hotel in the following week.

Louise has released four albums as I write this story, and she has gotten more than she could have ever imagined. But the most most striking thing about Louise is the smile and sparkling eyes that is always seen on her face anytime she sings.

Louise found her passion early in life, she pursued it in the midst of tragedy, she made it her purpose in life and now, she lives as happily as she could.

Why wouldn't you?

So, how do you find your passion or purpose?

- Do the things you love, and do what comes easy to you: this will require deep thought and you may even have to write things down, but I am sure that after the exercise, you will begin to see clearly what your passion is. What do you love to do, and still do very easily?

- Ask yourself, what you want the world to know about you: if you become very popular for one thing, what would that thing be? On the day you die, what do you want people to remember about you?

- Make the decisions about your life: many people find it hard to identify their passion because they have lived their lives with another person's manual. They have been told what to do at every junction of their lives, and now, all they know and have left are the lives of their advisers. Stand up for yourself and decide what you want to do.

- What has given you the most happiness in the world?: even if you have to go back to your childhood days to find an answer to this, do it. Passion is about enthusiasm which brings real happiness. Once you recall what made you the most happy in life, you don't have to look too far to identify your passion.

- Listen to positive people: sometimes, we don't see ourselves as truly and completely as other people see us. What do people tell you about your passion? What do they say they have noticed you do very well? When you get the answers, imagine yourself doing this things and see if it really makes you happy.

CHAPTER
Ten

Comfort Zone and Resistance to Change

"Life begins at the end of your comfort zone."

—Neale Donald Walsch

The comfort zone is a situation where you feel comfortable and your ability and determination is not put to test. It is a safe place in the mind which reduces stress and risk.

Literally, comfort zone is the temperature range where the human body is able to maintain a heat balance without shivering or sweating. Simply put, it is the normal secured place where no risks are taken and the easiest way out is taken.

Comfort zone is not necessarily laziness in physical work; it is laziness of the mind, mental laziness. It means you keep doing what is familiar and predictable and avoiding risk which is needed for you to grow. You cannot grow by staying in your comfort zone.

Some species of life shed their skin and moult before they grow. This is very instructive – you must put off the usual methods, the normal actions and the comfortable decisions if you want to grow.

The comfort zone makes you resist changes and forces you to stick to routines which have not yielded success in the past. Studies in psychology have shown that humans need an optimal level of anxiety in order to do great things. This optimal anxiety is just outside the mind's comfort zone and it increases our stress levels as well as our performance levels.

In order to protect itself against the unfamiliar and the uncertain, the mind resists change and tries to keep us in our comfort zones. It also tries to protect us from the necessary stress and optimal anxiety that will make us get better and achieve more.

Resisting change and living in the comfort zone brings the following:

- It reduces productivity: you easily lose your drive and ambition when you stay within the comfortable cocoon of your mind and only do the things that will not inspire you to do better.

- It kills creativity: it is only when you get out of your comfort zone that you can see new challenges and try to find solutions to new problems thereby increasing your creative ability.

- It limits success and makes you an underachiever: if you keep doing the things that do not require much ability and determination, you will never know the extent to which you can succeed, and you will never achieve more than your minimal effort.

- It hinders self-growth: like I have said before, you must get out of the comfortable place for you to grow and get better. It is how nature works. Consider a man who has worked in a company's local branch for ten years and refuses to leave that familiar space when given the opportunity to head to the headquarters; he will never become the head of such organization no matter how good he is or how impressive his resume is.

You will continue to miss opportunities and lose out of greater things until you decide to step out of your comfort zone and take some risk.

How to Get out of Comfort Zone

1. Do little things in different ways: spice things up a little bit in your life. When you take your bath, wash your legs first instead of the head, add something extra to your breakfast, take a different route when going home from work, shake up your routine and soon, these trivial actions will push you away from your comfort zone.

2. Think before making decisions: when you make decisions in the comfort zone, it is an automatic response you get, your mind doesn't spend time to consider too many things, you just take the decisions you took last week, last month or last year. But next time, try to think consciously and spend some moment to consider new ideas.

3. Trust yourself: allow yourself take risks and believe things will not go bad just because you are doing something that is usual. Have some confidence in your ability to succeed at new challenges.

4. Try something unfamiliar and new: change your wardrobe and buy different styles of clothes. Rearrange your office desk and learn a new programming language. These changes help the mind to be free of its laziness and leave the comfort zone.

5. Move towards your fear: most often, things you fear are things that threaten to break through your comfort zone. As you move towards your fear, you start to leave your comfort zone behind. Don't listen to the voice in your head which keeps telling you to stick to routine and not take risks; that voice will keep you down in life.

CHAPTER
Eleven

Self-Image/Identity

'You cannot let other people tell you who you are.
You have to decide that for yourself.'

—Unknown

The Cambridge Dictionary explains Self-image as 'the way a person feels about his or her personality, achievements and value to the society.' It is the way you perceive yourself. When you look in a mirror, who do you think is staring back at you? And what is the place of that person in the world? How does the world view that person?

Your own identity of yourself is far more important than the way people see you or what they think of you. Never allow that belief shake.

A fool who believes himself to be wise will have a much better quality of life than a wise men who thinks he is an idiot. Not because the fool is a better person, but because he will see love himself and be happy with his life.

This is why a positive self-image or self-identity is very powerful. It gives you strength and courage to handle the criticism of the world and gives you strength to face your life's challenges.

The game of football is very common in my town when I was growing up. I was in the field one evening when a scout came around and stopped us from playing.

'If you know you are a very good footballer, come to this right, and if you think you are not good enough yet, stay behind.' The scout announced.

I walked to his right side with seven other boys while about ten boys stayed behind. I must confess now that though I was a modest footballer as a young chap, I wasn't really excellent at it. But at the time of that announcement I used to think I was one of the best. And so I stepped out.

The man took down all our names without checking to see if we were as good as we said. He wasn't after the skill of football itself, he just wanted to see those who feel good about their abilities and believe they are good enough.

I think I was twelve at that time, and since then, I have learnt to never consider myself a lesser man.

I look at the pictures I took during my university days now, and I find myself wondering how I ever thought I was handsome. But it didn't matter, did it? So far I saw myself as handsome, I was handsome. And that positive image helped me through my time at school as it helped me walk confidently around campus without feelings ashamed or not good enough.

Your self-image or self-identity controls what you do, how you act, what you feel you deserve and what the society gives to you eventually.

While a weak self-image kills your self-esteem and makes you feel inadequate and weak, a strong self-image strengthens you, builds your confidence and helps you improve on your abilities as you take on challenges and live a better life.

Everyone is born with the same zero-level of self-image, but as we grow older, we begin to believe different things about ourselves and starting forming the idea of who we think we are.

Those who have parents who always put them down and tell them how bad they are may also start to convince themselves that they are bad and weak; thus, destroying their self-image.

But for the people who have been told as early as two years old that they are very good and lovely and beautiful, it wouldn't matter if they actually are all of these things; their self-image will be very strong.

And once formed, it is never easy to change your perception of yourself. You will need to convince yourself over and over again that you are better than you have always thought. And as you make some accomplishments in life, and achieve some success, your self-image becomes boosted and you see yourself in a new better light.

To improve your self-image, make a list of the following:

- the things you love about yourself
- the times you have overcome challenges
- the people you have helped
- your achievements
- the skills you have

If your life is a movie, and you are the director, how will you want your major character to be perceived? What roles will he take on? What must he do?

It is this mental movie that is playing in your life presently, and you must decide to change the plot and the take control of all that happens on the set of life.

Set your mind free and imagine yourself just as you want to be. There you are!

CHAPTER
Twelve

Master The Power of Habit

> *'Chains of habit are too light to be felt until*
> *they are too heavy to be broken'*
>
> **—Warren Buffet**

A habit is defined as an acquired behaviour or action that has been done often and regularly until it becomes almost or completely involuntary. It is a pattern of behavior that has been learned through frequent repetitive activity.

Studies suggest that 95 percent of a person's behaviour is determined by habit. Most habits are so unconscious that we don't even realize we are doing them.

This is why habits define our character, personality, feelings and decisions. Consider all the actions you have taken today, try to recall all the things you did. From waking up to the sound of an alarm, to getting into the bathroom and brushing your teeth, to dressing up and driving out, most of these activities were done out of habit.

Habits are powerful as they are critical to the way we live our lives.

How are habits formed?

A man broke down habit thus: the spelling is H-A-B-IT

IT is just a single thing that is mostly insignificant. A first attempt at something. It was just done once. People often say, 'No worries, "It" is my first time.'

BIT is a little more than once, though still in small amounts. The action has now been done just three or four times.

A BIT is now more that before. The quantity is increased, the action is repeated. 'It is just a bit of smoke'.

HABIT is then formed by constant repetition of it, bit and a bit until the mind learns to take the action on its own.

The brain works based on stimulus and response. When you do something for the first time, the stimulus must be connected to response before you decide to take an action. However, this connection becomes stronger as the same stimulus and response are repeated. And soon, this connection becomes permanent. If you repeat an action long enough, the brain picks up the action, creates the stimulus and decides the response all on its own. In the first stages where habit is formed, it may require a trigger. But when habit grows to become addiction, even without a trigger, an action is taken.

Habit determines destiny. A student who has the habit of waking up in the night to study his books will get success while a student who has the habit of sleeping through the class will hardly get success. The same can be said of every other sphere of life.

Both bad habits and good habits are formed in the same way. You have to decide which of these you want to rule over your life.

While good habits help you become financially wiser, be on time, have good health and lifestyle, and become generally productive and happy, bad habits keep you from your goal, keeps you in mediocrity, pushes you from other people and destroy your relationship.

Make a checklist of all you did daily for a week, study the things that were done out of habit, and consider if these habits are pushing you towards a better life, or pushing people away.

CHAPTER
Thirteen

Attachment

'Attachment is the source of all suffering.
You only lose what you cling to.'

—Buddha

Attachment is a deep and lasting emotional connection or bond to someone or something. It is the formation of bond from one person to another person. Sometimes, we can also feel attached to things.

Examples of attachment is seen between siblings that always want to be together, a wife that longs for her husband, a child that wants her mother, a woman who wants to see her hometown, and a man who cannot find is mobile phone.

The attachment theory was proposed by John Bowlby and James Robertson in the 1950s. The theory explains the relationship between a child and a parent, especially the mother. Psychologists have presented two main theories which are important in forming attachments. One theory believes that attachment is a set of learned behaviours while another theory suggests that attachment in babies had been biologically pre-engineered to for attachments with others in order to survive.

- Attachment always requires deep emotions and it can dictate how we feel. A child may never stop crying until he sees his mother, a woman may not stop crying until she sees her child. This is why I see attachment as a key we give to people so they can have access to our emotions. You must be careful who you give this key.

- Attachment impacts relationships and decide the level of happiness. When you stay close to those things or people you are attached to, you feel very happy. This is why long-distance relationships sometimes don't work when one of the partners stops feeling the other party is too detached.

- Attachment is involved in addiction. When you feel too attached to a particular thing, it can be to the extent that you may feel incomplete and unhappy until that thing is near. A person's addiction can be to get his phone into his hands, while another might be the need to swallow some pills. In any case, the happiness has been tied to a substance.

- It also limits us by hindering us from being at our best independent of another person or substance. When an athlete cannot perform until he takes a certain substance, what will happen to him when such substance is taken away? When a person you are attached to disappoint as most humans do, will you still be able to achieve your goals?

Attachment and Detachment

Detachment is the separation that may be necessary for you to get some levels of achievement. You must learn to detach yourself from toxic people and toxic substances.

You must let go of the past, let go of beliefs that don't serve you, let go of your attachment to outcome, let go of relationships that do not serve you, and let go of heart breaks and break ups.

Detachment is important because the truth is that 'Things you own will own you'. It doesn't mean you cannot enjoy things, it only means that while you enjoying everything, do not be controlled them

When you live with detachment, you become independent of your attachments. You may continue the relationship, but you have enough strength to do without them.

How to live without attachment and master the art of letting go

1. Understand that nothing really lasts forever
2. Always remember that you have the keys to your heart
3. Never think that you can control other people's actions
4. Master the art of forgiveness, for others and yourself
5. Give up on people who don't matter
6. Always keep in mind that life goes on without you
7. Don't expect too much from people
8. Express your feelings fully until you are free of them
9. Stay in the moment and enjoy the present
10. Have no hatred for anyone

CHAPTER
Fourteen

Paradigm, Emotions, Focus and Will-Power

In a bid to have better understanding of how the world works, we acquire knowledge about it as we grow. A paradigm is way of understanding and organizing this knowledge and condensing sensory information. Our paradigms also affect the way we interpret actions and what we think about others.

It is very important for each person to master his paradigm as it guides expectations and determines that things we question and the things we accept as true. Thus, your personal paradigm impacts all areas of your life: health care, money, relationship, what we do, want, have, become and achieve.

Factors that influence and create paradigms

Two main factors that influence paradigm are Genetic and environment or culture. That is, what you are born with, and the ones you pick up as you grow.

Heredity or genetic:

We all are born with five core limbic drives or programs, no matter what nomenclature we use to describe them; whether we call them needs, drives, motivations or inner forces.

In the absence of the conscious experience of these limbic drives, the behaviour of a man or a group can be seen as manifestation of these drives.

The five drives are:

1. Sexual limbic drive: the sex organs and the hormones can motivate strongly as our body drives us to seek sexual pleasure.

2. Survival or security: the basic instinct of survival is another thing that drives humans and motivates them to act. We want to stay alive and feel secured.

3. Power: the need for power is borne out of the feeling of self-importance. People pursue power in order to control other people or just to feel better about themselves.

4. Territorial: humans generally want to own their space, and they will do everything to protect that space when they get it.

5. Nurturance: the need to care for people we love, protect and provide for them is another strong motivator of humans.

We are all born with different intensity levels of these drives. Some may be born with high power drive and low survival and nurturance. Some may have high survival and low power.

These drives are deeply rooted in us although they may manifest at different stages of our lives. For example, attachment to parents or mother is expressed by infants i.e survival drive is active when we are born and then comes power and sexual drive.

Effect of environment: besides the drives we are born with, we gather knowledge as we learn and alter the things we have always believed to be our motivator. A lot of persons born with a high sexual drive have learnt to control the urge and redirect their energy to getting power. This may have been as a result of an experience that compelled them to change. Human beings change their beliefs and motivations based on their experiences.

INABILITY TO CONTROL NEGATIVE EMOTIONS

Negative emotions are the feelings you have which are unpleasant and seek the destruction of yourself or another person. Everyone experiences negative emotions from time to time, the only difference is that some have learnt to control such emotions, some others live in the negative emotions.

Jealousy, envy, guilt, regret, hatred, revenge, anger and sadness are some examples of negative emotions. These emotions are not learnt or acquired, they are often provoked by changes in the environment which get to the brain as stimuli and what we feel as these emotions are the responses our brain gives.

Emotions generally differ from person to person; this is why what makes one man angry may just make another man sad or guilty. Our past experiences have a lot to do with our negative emotions and how we respond to them.

Emotions and brain:

Human brain can be divided into three regions that sequentially developed with evolution.

Lowest region or the *Reptilian brain* is responsible for balance, breathing, digestion, and involuntary activities.

Middle region or the *Limbic brain* is responsible forsocial behaviours and emotions.

Front region or *Neocortex* is the seat of reason and intellect

The limbic brain contain instincts, drives, urges, impulses that generate emotions and social

behaviours; it has the ability to highjack the neocortex and reptilian brain. Have you ever gotten angry at a situation and you later realize you could have handled the situation better if you hadn't gotten angry? This happens because your limbic system has highjacked your neocortex.

No negative emotion is ever felt by the person you are directing the emotion to. You are the one who bears these negative feelings until it poisons you and affects you health, relationship, success and motivation.

How to Master these negative emotions?

- Take control of the situation
- Speak your mind on time

- Think logically before you act
- Put yourself in the other person's shoes and try to be understanding
- Practise gratitude
- Don't keep it bottled up
- Tell someone about it
- Focus on yourself

FOCUS

"I focus on one thing and one thing only-
And that's trying to win as many championships as I can."

—Kobe Bryant

Focus is the concentration of attention and energy on one thing.

The human mind is best with the ability to take on many things at a time, but this ability can work against us if we do not learn to focus. There are levels of success which a person may never get to until he drops other things and concentrate on that one thing. Just consider the people who made real breakthrough and are popular; all of them are popular for one thing. There is a major challenge they took on and overcame; a single work they did and master; one talent they harnessed and became great at.

I am not saying it is impossible to do more than one thing in one's lifetime. No. What I am saying is, you must spend your time and energy on a thing at a time; once this one thing is achieved, you can then move on to other things, focus on them and achieve them.

A good footballer can also be good at academics, but he must not be thinking about his academics when on the field of play, and he must not think of football when inside the class; otherwise, he would fail at both.

That is the power of focus. It is illustrated by the saying, 'if given enough time, even water can break a rock if it keeps dropping on a particular point.'

Once you can channel your energy on one goal, your probability of achieving that goal doubles.

Focus is especially important in this age of social media where distractions are numerous and so many other activates are calling for your time. But a person who is focused will keep his gaze on his target, run at it, and win.

Why is it important to have focus?

1. It increases productivity
2. It allows you see more clearly
3. It keeps your mind sharp
4. It makes you work faster
5. It requires less stress

Methods to improve Focus

1. Learn the art of Meditation
2. Learn how to Prioritize
3. Set a schedule and follow it
4. Eat well and rest when you should
5. Set clear goals
6. Get teammates
7. Solve critical questions with your brain

WILLPOWER

"People do not lack strength; they lack will."

—Victor Hugo

Willpower is defined as the ability to control your own thoughts and the way you behave; it is also the ability to restrain impulses and say No when you know you should.

You need to have a strong willpower in order to resist the voices in your head, and suggestions from people around who are telling you to quit, give up and leave.

If your life is the fist, willpower is the muscle that keeps the fist tightened and strong.

When a soldier is standing at attention and a fly perches on his nose, it takes absolute willpower to keep his hands by his side and restrain the urge to wipe the face.

When a musician is booed on stage, it takes willpower to stand straight, face the crowd and keep singing.

When a child makes a mistake for the one hundredth time, it takes willpower for the parent to hold back his tongue or hands from abuse.

When a boss derides you and blames you for his own mistakes, it takes willpower for you to keep your mouth shut and let it go.

When your partner says something wrong, it takes willpower for you not to stare him in the face and release fire and brimstone from your lips.

When you have tried everything you could, and still fail, it takes willpower to try again and refuse to quit.

You cannot put the lessons and methods written in this book to practice without willpower.

There is no success that comes without willpower.

But an average human mind often battles between resisting the urges of giving in.

And the truth is, the one you feed more grows more. I mean, if you keep giving in to your urges, you will have very weak willpower. But if you keep resisting your urges and the voices, your willpower will grow stronger and stronger. Each victory over your mind makes you stronger.

Methods to improve willpower

- Learn to withstand pressure
- Stick to the plan
- Get more sleep to recharge
- Eat, exercise, meditate
- Postpone your pleasures
- Get firmer control over your life